Land Reform
and Economic Development
in China

VICTOR D. LIPPIT

Land Reform
and Economic Development
in China

A STUDY OF INSTITUTIONAL CHANGE
AND DEVELOPMENT FINANCE

INTERNATIONAL ARTS AND SCIENCES PRESS, INC. WHITE PLAINS, N.Y.

Library of Congress Catalog Card Number: 74-15391

International Standard Book Number: 0-87332-064-6

Printed in the United States of America

Second Printing

For Noriko

Contents

Preface

The question of development finance in underdeveloped countries is ultimately one of the use of the surplus: how can a significant part of that share of national income above a nation's culturally determined subsistence requirements be channeled into investment? In every society an elaborate system of claims on the surplus exists, whether as a material expression of the fealty owed to elders and chiefs in tribal society or the rent, interest, and profits due the owners of capital in capitalist society. These systems of claims are ordinarily so deeply imbedded in the social structure that any effort to redirect the income flows associated with them into socially fruitful investment channels will be severely constrained. Only when the existing claims are eliminated through the revolutionary transformation of society does an opportunity arise for massive redirection of the income flows that compose the surplus into development finance.

Although revolution creates a unique opportunity to increase the share of national income devoted to capital formation, the opportunity is easily missed. New patterns of social organization emerge together with new claims on the surplus; these claims rapidly acquire the sanctions of orthodox practice. At the same time, much of the revolutionary élan is associated with the vision of the redistribution of the surplus in favor of the revolutionary classes, and to restrain such redistribution so as to increase the investment share when revolutionary efforts are crowned with success is a difficult matter. Thus appropriate policy measures must be chosen if an underdeveloped country is to seize the opportunity to initiate or accelerate its modernization which revolution creates.

The experience of China in raising her national savings-investment ratio by taking advantage of the situation created when revolution forced the traditional claimants on the nation's economic surplus to relinquish their claims is perhaps the most significant in world history, both in scope and in the clarity of the issues involved. It is this experience of China and the central role played by the land reform in particular that I analyze in detail here. Only a complete tracing of the manner in which the surplus share of national income was diverted to the financing of new investment can clarify the role of the revolution in China's economic development. But while this study focuses on China, the methodology and analysis are of more general applicability, bearing directly on central issues in the disciplines of economic history and economic development. Thus it is my hope that besides serving to illuminate the process of historical transformation in China, this study will offer some suggestions to those concerned with historical or contemporary processes of change in other countries.

Chapter Two is devoted entirely to a study of the property share in the rural sector of the traditional economy of China. While the concept of property share depends on the source of income flows and that of surplus on their use, for most purposes the two concepts are interchangeable. I have chosen to conduct the analysis in terms of income shares because the concept lends itself to somewhat more precise definition and because the available data lend themselves more readily to treatment within this framework. Nevertheless, my treatment of the property share ultimately reflects my approach to and concern with the surplus. As it is the size and disposition of the surplus that determines the character and direction of change of any society, the analysis undertaken here of the redirection of China's surplus from luxury consumption to investment will serve to clarify the whole process of economic and social change in modern China.

The methodology I have devised for treating this question with regard to China is perfectly general and can be applied with equal validity to the present or historical analysis of the capital share or surplus in other countries. Perhaps the most obvious material for a case study of this sort is provided by the Indian economy, although analysis along these lines is of utmost importance in all of the underdeveloped countries, to clarify both their present situation and the options available to them. Thus the issues I am ultimately concerned with are basic ones in economic development: how can the capital share or surplus present in all underdeveloped countries be estimated and what are the processes by which the traditional patterns of income and spending flows can be altered to increase the share of national income devoted to investment? It is, then, with the dual purpose of analyzing the experience of China at a critical juncture in modern Chinese history and of contributing to the analysis of the role of the surplus in economic development that I have undertaken this study.

I would like to thank Hugh Patrick, Carl Riskin, Raymond Powell, Robert Dernberger, Stephen Resnick, Dwight Perkins, and Ben Stavis for their many useful criticisms. Each of them read the entire manuscript and made substantive suggestions for its improvement; I am especially indebted to Hugh Patrick and Carl Riskin for their close readings and detailed critiques of the text. I would also like to thank Professor John Lossing Buck and Mr. Ardron B. Lewis for their assistance in unravelling some of the mysteries with which the nonparticipant in history is invariably confronted. In particular, I would like to express my appreciation to Professor Shigeru Ishikawa of the Institute of Economic Research, Hitotsubashi University, whose analysis of the work helped to clarify some of the basic conceptual issues. Above all, I would like to express my intellectual debt to Noriko Mizuta Lippit, whose perception had the most influence on the intellectual framework within which this work was conceived.

Victor D. Lippit

Riverside, California
June 1974

Land Reform
and Economic Development
in China

CHAPTER ONE

Property ownership, class relations, and the national savings-investment ratio

Following the success of the communist-led revolution in 1949, the economic institutions of China were revamped on a vast scale. Coincident with and dependent upon these changes was a sharp increase in the share of net domestic expenditure devoted to (net) investment, from about 1.7% in 1933 to more than 20% in the First Five-Year Plan period, 1953-1957. (1) While there is no dispute over the fact that the investment ratio increased substantially, and while there has been a fairly comprehensive discussion of the structural changes which the Chinese economy underwent in the 1950s, no attempt to link these two systematically has yet been made. The purpose of this study is, in general terms, to explore the relationship between institutional change and economic development in China, and more specifically, to quantify, to the extent that it is possible, the impact of one of the most important of these changes, land reform, on the share of national income available for investment in China.

Land reform was initially instituted in much of the liberated area of China prior to October 1949, but swept over most of the country in the 1950-1952 period. It involved principally the redistribution of land from landlords and, to a lesser extent, rich peasants to poor and landless peasants. In all, some 700 million mou (2) were redistributed, with the total changing hands constituting approximately 44% of China's arable land area. (3) By 1952 net domestic investment as a proportion of net domestic

3

expenditure had climbed to 15.4% from the barely more than
nominal investment rates which had prevailed in traditional
China, and the ratio climbed steeply again to 20.23% in 1953. (4)
As my argument will make clear in the course of this study, a
sizable, although not predominant, share of the increase in national saving needed to finance this increase in investment can
be attributed to the impact of the land reform.

There are a number of a priori reasons, aside from the historical correlation between land reform and the rising investment rate, for supposing that this change in property ownership
might have contributed to increasing the investment share of
national income. These can be clarified by considering them
together with some of the more general aspects of the investment problem.

To increase the share of investment in an economy, either
some existing consumption must be sacrificed or a substantial
share of incremental output must be devoted to investment.
The latter is often unrealistic as a method of initiating economic development in that it assumes that economic growth will
provide the necessary conditions for economic growth. (5) The
former method has often been objected to on the grounds that
in a poor country it is not reasonable to expect people to save
very much. (6) This objection tends to overlook the fact that
even in poor countries not everyone is poor — and that the consumption (or saving) function is dependent on relative as well
as on absolute income.

In all countries the unequal distribution of property ownership is a major factor in the unequal distribution of income. (7)
In underdeveloped countries, with weakly developed industry,
the ownership of agricultural land is ordinarily one of the major forms of property ownership. Such countries can be divided
into two broad categories: those in which the landlords are of
an entrepreneurial type and those in which they are not. In
reality, these categories represent the extremes of an entire
range. England and Japan provide historical examples in which
the enterprising landlord invested both in agriculture and

outside it to contribute to the economic development of the country.

If the property owner (landlord) is an investor, then his higher-than-average income may contribute to increasing the rate of capital formation. This is especially true if most people can be persuaded that his special position is the reward of special virtue (Social Darwinism) or if the power of the domestic police and paramilitary authorities is sufficient to keep those who would question his special status in line. Then both the investment and social stability requirements for development would be met, and one could expect a positive correlation between the degree of income inequality and the share of national income devoted to investment.

If, however, the property owner (landlord) uses his above-average income for above-average (luxury) consumption (8) rather than investment, or to finance the dissaving of others through land purchase, high-interest loans, and so forth, the income inequality associated with property ownership would make no contribution to development. To the contrary, it would prove a hindrance. The Chinese landlord appears to have fallen in this latter category. Net investment in agriculture was close to zero in traditional China (9), and numerous case observations confirm the noninvesting behavior of the typical landlord. (10) Ordinarily, where land was rented out, the tenant provided most of the capital stock. (11) The failure to invest vigorously in agriculture need not be attributed to the financial or moral incapacity of landlowners but can properly be ascribed to the low returns China's traditional agricultural economy was capable of affording in the absence of large-scale complementary investments — in roads for example — or major technological breakthroughs. (12) The landowner's behavior should not be understood as economically irrational: increasing the nation's capital stock did not typically provide the highest returns available to the individual "investor."

There are five principal ways in which the drain of resources into the financing of dissaving and luxury consumption might

Luxury spending [handwritten margin note]

have been halted under this condition: (1) taxation, (2) socialization, (3) the provision of attractive investment opportunities, (4) the redistribution of land to reduce tenancy and the inequality of ownership and income, and (5) institutional change to eliminate the social and economic conditions which brought about dissaving. Brief consideration of each of these possibilities will help to clarify the alternatives available.

High agricultural taxes may have disincentive effects regarding labor inputs, innovation, and the marketed share of farm output — although each of these may be overcome in part through a well-designed tax system. (13) In the specific Chinese context, however, by far the overriding consideration ruling out an increase in taxation (either through tight administration or higher rates) large enough to have had a major impact on the national savings ratio was the regime's reliance on the support of the (larger) landowners. This reliance was not just a matter of the Kuomintang's requiring support to stay in office but concerned its very capacity to govern: the Chinese gentry, including principally landowners, dominated rural China, and the Kuomintang could rule through it or not at all. It simply could not act in a way that disregarded the most basic interests of this group. In fact, corruption, tax farming, exorbitant special levies, and unequal distribution of the tax burden due to the ability of the well-placed to avoid payment altogether (14) made efforts to reduce taxation the order of the day in the 1930s. (15) While after 1940 there was some increase in agricultural taxation associated with wartime conditions, its magnitude was not and could not have been such as to make a fundamental dent in the accumulation problem.

In one sense, socialization might have provided the neatest solution to the problem of restraining luxury consumption and dissaving. By transferring property ownership and its associated claims on output from private hands to the state, the private predilection for luxury consumption and pecuniary gain might have been replaced by a public one for investment and the social conditions which promoted dissaving transformed

(see the discussion below). If implemented immediately, such
a program might well have been attended by a good many disincentive effects, however, and thrown farm management into
confusion. (This is indeed what happened when oversized communes were formed in excessive haste a decade later.) Perhaps of more importance, the poor and middle peasants on
whose political support the new regime relied would not have
been as enthusiastic about such a program as they were about
the "land to the tillers" land reform program actually adopted.

To talk of the provision of more attractive investment opportunities implies a greater degree of public control over private
investment than in fact existed. The problems which would have
attended any such effort, moreover, were not marginal in nature.
What was required was a complete transformation of the economic environment: not only massive complementary investments of the social overhead capital type, but the conditions of
social stability which only popular support or massive terror
could bring. The Kuomintang was not strong enought to impose
its rule on China's vast countryside, and it was not until its
rule was reduced to the single province of Taiwan that it found
itself capable of imposing stability. (16) With China's traditional social structure collapsing under the impact of the twentieth century, it was beyond the power of the Kuomintang to
provide the stability upon which long-term, productivity-
increasing investments depend.

The redistribution and equalization of land holdings under
the land reform program did in fact eliminate the luxury consumption associated with the ownership of an above-average
amount of land. It also eliminated the lending capacity associated with unusual wealth, canceled outstanding debts, and for-
bade high-interest loans, thus reducing the dissaving to which
these contributed. Since land ownership remained private,
however, a question remains concerning the extent to which
public policy was successful in extricating a portion of the incremental income which the poor peasants especially received
as a consequence of the land reform.

The poor peasant beneficiaries of the land reform in China may be presumed to have had a high marginal propensity to consume and, as Donnithorne points out (17), a high income elasticity of demand for food in particular. Thus the more equitable distribution of income cannot in itself be responsible for increasing saving and investment. Prior to 1955, when the collectivization of agriculture took place, then, the increase in the national savings-investment ratio which may be ascribed to the land reform depended on the extent to which peasant efforts to increase consumption were restricted through agricultural taxation or manipulation of the terms of trade between agriculture and industry. Viewed from this standpoint, any increase in peasant consumption may be regarded as a leakage; the task of the government was to extract as much of the windfall income which land reform brought to the peasants as possible, under the constraints of assuring the basic consumption requirements of the peasantry and not harming production incentives or alienating the class whose interests it represented.

In considering institutional change to eliminate the social and economic conditions which brought about dissaving, two principal considerations immediately come to the fore. First, the inequality of income distribution in traditional China promoted dissaving. (18) This is not merely a matter of the consumption demonstration effect, which typically makes it impossible for all but those in the top income strata to have positive net saving even in developed countries, but of the marginal quality of life in traditional China as well. People living right at the subsistence level in normal times could survive physically only by dissaving at the time of a crop failure or other calamity, and calamities have appeared with distressing frequency in modern Chinese history. The greater the inequality of income distribution, the greater the number of people who shared this marginal status.

According to the conventional view, unequal income distribution increases the savings potential of a society because only the rich can afford to save. Under certain circumstances this may indeed be the case, although there is no assurance that the potential will be realized even if it is there. In China, however, the inequality does not appear to have enhanced saving: the poor were too poor to save and the rich lacked incentives to do so. Moreover, the limited saving of the rich was largely offset by the dissaving of the poor: the rich bought up the land of the poor and made loans to them, enabling them temporarily to spend more than their current income. As long as the rich, attracted by high interest and the income, status, and security of owning land, used their surplus income to make transfer payments of this kind, national saving would be discouraged; for with few exceptions, only those in dire straits, needing funds for emergency consumption, would borrow or give up their land. The tendency toward increased tenancy and absentee landownership was also institutionally inimical to increased saving and investment, because the tenant was responsible for most of the investment and had little incentive to improve permanently land that was not his.

In addition to the negative influence on saving exerted by inequality, the "familial individualism" of traditional Chinese society also discouraged saving and promoted dissaving. In the midst of a harsh environment and lacking any public authority which could provide succor in time of distress, the Chinese naturally depended upon his family. Under such circumstances, rituals which served to strengthen family bonds held a prominent place in traditional Chinese society. (19) As much as a year's income might be spent on the wedding of a son, obligating the young couple to the bridegroom's parents. Funerals were elaborate and costly. Family-strengthening ceremonies such as these were commonly a form of conspicuous consumption but warranted high expenditure as well because of the preeminent role of the family in securing and insuring the individual's existence. In a society where such insurance is a public concern, the economic rationale which underlay the elaborate family rituals would disappear, and with it the substantial dissaving which supported them. (20) Thus institutional changes which promoted a more equal distribution of income and those which promoted a transfer of the responsibility for assuring the life of the individual from private hands to society could both be expected to reduce dissaving. Changes of precisely this sort were brought about by the land reform in the context of the establishment of the new socialist regime in China.

The land reform, which distributed private hoards as well as rented land, made the financing of elaborate rituals with either one's own or borrowed funds practically impossible. The existence of the poorest sixty percent of the rural population became less precarious, and a small part of the increased tax revenues which the land reform made possible sufficed to finance the state's assumption of the obligation to provide relief when personal or natural catastrophe did strike. Finally, the peasant associations which carried out the land redistribution provided means of mobilizing public opinion against those who attempted to maintain expensive rituals. This is by no means an insignificant consideration, as the pressure of peer-group opinion is a major factor governing individual behavior in China.

For the reasons I have outlined in the Preface, this study focuses mainly on income flows and therefore the property share. Just as national product can be analyzed in terms of end products rather than in terms of income flows, however, the changes brought by the land reform can be analyzed in terms of the changes in income use rather than in terms of the changes in income flows. The income uses that correspond to the property share of national income make up the "surplus."

The central notion of the concept "surplus" is that a certain portion of the total output of goods and services in an economy is not necessary to maintain the living standard of a nation at the minimum level of decency and comfort which its history, material resources, and culture determine. The surplus is, in essence, the difference between national income and that portion of the national income needed to maintain the entire population at this culturally determined subsistence level. Depending on how the concept is to be applied, however, a number of variations from this basic definition are possible.

In using the term surplus, I refer to the difference between national output, modified to include the potential output of property owners who do not work, and essential or subsistence expenditures. (21) In regarding the concept of surplus as interchangeable with the property share, I am assuming that subsistence income is approximated by labor income plus the income of peasant proprietors, where labor income includes the potential output of nonworking property owners. Clarification of the rationale underlying this treatment should also help to clarify my reasons for treating all of property income — not just the share of it that sustains luxury consumption — as representing a potential source of investment finance.

Since a portion of property income may be used to sustain the essential consumption of property owners, the question may be raised whether all of property income can properly be associated with the surplus. Several considerations argue strongly in favor of such treatment. Many landlords had other occupations — they were pawnshop owner-managers, merchants, civil and military officials, and so forth. For those with labor sources of income, property ownership need not be regarded as providing the basis for essential consumption. This still leaves a substantial number of landlords without significant alternative sources of income.

If we assume the same average physical and mental capacity to hold true among property owners as among the rest of the population, however, the property-owning portion of the population can achieve the same labor income as the rest of the population by working. China's land reform created the necessity of and condition for such work by expropriating rented land and reallocating to former landlords an amount of land equal to the average per capita holding in the region in question. This in turn raises the question of whether the additions to the work force would lower the marginal productivity of labor and prevent the former property owners from earning a subsistence wage.

Normally, such an effect might be expected because the quantities of land and capital were fixed in the short run. Since each person received an approximately equal share of land, however, any reduction in average product would be spread equally over the whole population and not affect solely the marginal entrants to the labor force. Furthermore, the quantitative impact of former landlords entering the agricultural labor force cannot have been very great. Landlords constituted only 3% of the rural population prior to the land reform, and not all of them lacked alternative sources of income. (22) Even assuming the size of the rural labor force increased by the full 3%, the increase was spread over more than three years and compares with a rate of population increase of slightly over 2% annually in the early 1950s. Such an increase cannot be expected to have significantly affected average product. Moreover, to the extent that peasants were drawn from the land to engage in the new capital construction and other economic activities stimulated by the revolutionary government, the (average) productivity-reducing effect of the added labor brought about by the land reform would be offset.

For all of these reasons, I consider it a reasonable approximation to include the essential consumption of property owners as part of the rural surplus. This does not imply that property owners were deprived of such consumption by the land reform, simply that they had to finance it, like everyone else, by working. This assumption makes it possible to treat the entire property income in the rural sector as surplus. The property share and the surplus are, then, two sides of the same coin, and the opportunity cost of diverting the income flows that made up the property share was the components of the surplus they had financed.

The impact of the land reform on saving, then, is to be found in its diversion of funds within the agricultural sector from luxury consumption and dissaving. But the reduction of these leakages did not in itself guarantee that new ones would not appear: it remains necessary to determine what part of the

diverted funds found its way into investment. To investigate
the diversion of funds from luxury consumption and dissaving
and to determine what part of the funds thus diverted found its
way into investment, a somewhat circuitous route must be followed. In the absence of adequate direct data on consumption
and dissaving, it is possible to look instead at the property income which sustained luxury consumption and financed dissaving. This indirectness is not, however, all to the bad. It makes
possible viewing the impact of institutional change in property
rights all the more directly. Moreover, the estimate of the
capital or property share in the rural sector (including, and
with the focus on, land rent) which it requires — and which
forms the theme of Chapter Two — casts light on a relatively
unexplored area of Chinese economic history. This estimate
provides the most useful basis for evaluating the impact of the
post-1949 institutional changes on the corresponding income
flows.

By distributing the landlords' land among the poor and landless peasants, the new regime made possible an increase in
income among these groups. A portion of the increase could
then be taxed away, either directly or indirectly, leaving a net
increase in the income of those on whose support the new regime relied, while at the same time increasing its tax and other
revenues from the agricultural sector. These revenues could
then in turn be used to finance capital construction projects.
As Alexander Eckstein, who treats the 1952 agricultural tax in
kind as nationalized land rent, has argued, the land reform

> provided a vehicle by which the land rent could be appro-
> priated by the state for its own use. Inasmuch as land rent
> in China was mostly dissipated in consumption, conspicu-
> ous and otherwise, in hoarding, and after 1936 also in cap-
> ital flight, expropriation of this rent furnished a means for
> raising the level of investment in the economy. (23)

It is precisely this assertion concerning the impact of the land

reform on the investment level which is the major subject of
my investigation and for which I provide the statistical under-
pinnings in the following chapters. As the analysis of Chapter
Three will make clear, the land reform made a sizable but not
predominant contribution to financing China's economic development, with most of the rerouted income streams winding up
in the form of higher consumption on the part of the peasants
who received them.

While efforts to increase investment also played a major role
in spurring Chinese collectivization in the mid-1950s, all but a
minor part of the increase in the national savings-investment
ratio took place well before the collectivization drive. Since
it is this increase that I am principally concerned with, I do
not treat collectivization in great detail. Still, I shall touch
briefly on the connection between collectivization and the national savings ratio, because it both clarifies the historical
role of the land reform and completes the picture of the relationship between institutional change in agriculture and the
financing of economic development in China. Clarification of
this relationship may also provide insight into the rationale
behind some of the major policy changes which occurred and
their timing, making more clear the whole process of change
and growth in China in the 1950s.

In the last analysis, the major problem of development finance is that of raising the saving ratio in the entire economy.
This may be done by taking measures to increase private saving or government saving. While the government can undertake
institutional reorganization of the private sector in order to increase incentives to invest, its control over the amount and
direction of such investment is inherently less complete than
its control over the funds which it dispenses itself. This fact,
together with no less significant ideological considerations, led
the new Chinese regime to rely primarily on government saving
to increase the overall saving ratio. There were, in turn, two
basic means utilized to increase public saving: increasing tax
receipts and raising the profits of government enterprises. In

one sense these two amount to the same thing, since appropriate price adjustments could convert one into the other, or obli-
gatory payments to the state of the profits of state enterprises
might be treated as tax payments. To obtain the full contribution of the agricultural sector to government income and hence
to development finance, the profits or taxes which the government derives from firms trading with the agricultural sector
must be taken into account as well as the more direct receipts. (24)

In short, the first step in assessing the actual contribution
of the institutional change in China to development finance (via
an increase in central government revenues), is to estimate
the quantitative importance of the relevant pre-1949 property
share components. This will provide the basis for estimates
of the extent to which and the manner in which the income
streams which previously flowed to the owners of private property were diverted to the central government.

For an analysis of the impact of institutional change it is essential to provide some picture of the situation of the Chinese
economy prior to the time when the economic reforms were
put into effect. Thus I have incorporated some background material of this sort in my discussion in Chapter Two, while including in the Statistical Appendix the relevant national income
data, the receipts and expenditures of the government, and other
data which indicate the historical context within which the subsequent institutional changes took place. In order to abstract
from the economic disturbances associated with the war against
Japan and the civil war, and because the period around 1933 is
the only period for which sufficient data are available, I have
used it as the prewar basis for comparisons. Before treating
this material, however, some further theoretical elaboration
of the hypothesis under consideration should help to clarify the
subsequent analysis.

The theoretical framework

The central hypothesis at issue here is that the reduction of consumption previously attributable to the owners of land and other property in the agricultural sector, together with a reduction in the dissaving which their lending activities promoted, were principal factors in making possible the increase in the national savings ratio. The principal relationships may be expressed in equation form in the following manner:

A. Income Relationships Prior to the Land Reform

$$
\begin{align}
Y_a &= .89Q \tag{1} \\
Y_a &= Y_t + Y_p \tag{2} \\
Y_t &= rQ + r'Q + iL_{tp} = C_t + S_t + M_t \tag{3} \\
Y_p &= (.89 - r - r')Q - iL_{tp} = C_p + S_p + M_s \tag{4} \\
S_t &= \Delta L_{tp} + N \tag{5} \\
S_p &= -\Delta L_{tp} \tag{6}
\end{align}
$$

where: Y_a = net value added in agriculture;

Q = gross value of output in agriculture;

Y_t = personal income of property owners in the agricultural sector, excluding peasant proprietors;

Y_p = personal income of peasants, including peasant proprietors;

r = the share of rent in the gross value of agricultural output;

r' = the share of the gross value of agricultural output produced on land worked by full-time hired labor above and beyond the cost of such labor;

i = the interest rate on loans to peasants;

L_{tp} = loans from property owners to peasants, amount outstanding;

C_t = property-owner consumption;

S_t = property-owner saving;

C_p = peasant consumption;

S_p = peasant saving;

M = removals (the command over resources which is removed from income recipients in the agricultural sector via taxation or government control over the terms of trade with the industrial sector);

M_t = property-owner removals;

M_p = peasant removals;

N = landlord saving other than the net increase in loans to peasants.

Equation (1) is based on the estimate by Ta-chung Liu and Kung-chia Yeh for 1933, in 1933 prices, of a gross value of output for agriculture of 21.17 billion yuan and a net value added of 18.76 billion. (25) In that year, the former figure is Q and the latter Y_a. As there was no substantial change in agricultural technology or organization during the 1930s or 1940s, any deviations from the 1933 relationship will have been minor: I have, accordingly, treated it as constant during this period.

Equation (2) allocates the value added in the agricultural sector to property owners (principally landowners) and those who do farm work (I have called them peasants, but farm laborers as well are meant to be included in this category). This is not meant to be a full analytic breakdown of the returns to property and labor, since Y_p includes the income received by peasant proprietors, with no attempt to isolate and exclude the imputed returns to land. Since Y_t and Y_p represent personal income, I am assuming that governmental and net intersectoral transfers were unimportant. This assumption is not wholly warranted because urban residents and émigrés were sending remittances to their families in the countryside. I have felt justified in making it because there is no way to ascertain the exact level of such remittances (although it is certain that they decreased sharply in the 1940s), and their contribution to personal income in the countryside did not constitute a substantial share of the total. (26) This exclusion of the (net) transfer component of personal income means that Y_t and Y_p are slightly understated:

this is equally true in equations (3) and (4).

Equations (3) and (4) show the sources (left side) and uses (right side) of property owner and peasant income respectively. Y_t and Y_p are defined as personal income after income transfers within the agricultural sector: as a positive term in equation (3) and a negative term in equation (4), iL_{tp} (interest payments from peasants to property owners) appears as an increment to the income of property owners and as a reduction from the income of peasants. In equation (3) the income of property owners is divided into land rent (rQ), farm business profits ($r'Q$), and interest (iL_{tp}). The consumption and saving components of the uses of income are quite conventional, but the third term on the right side, M_t, bears a word of explanation. The term "removals" is meant to reflect the fact that government control over the terms of trade between the agricultural and industrial sectors may function just like taxation in limiting income recipients' purchasing power. Prior to 1949, however, the means for such control did not exist, so that M_t and M_p represent exclusively the personal tax payments of property owners and peasants.

In equation (4) peasant income is treated as what remains after the return to property (realized by landlords and by those who hire others to farm for them), together with the net interest paid to property owners, is deducted from the net value added in agriculture. Most farm loans were made for consumption purposes (27), and that this term is iL_{tp} reflects the fact that loans were typically made by property owners to peasants, with the interest payments moving, in due course, in the opposite direction.

Equation (5) shows property-owner saving reflected in the net change in loans to peasants and all other uses (N). These other uses were typically "nonproductive" investments such as hoarding and luxury housing (28), including that for owner use. The nature and level of investment undertaken by property owners is discussed in a separate section of Chapter Two. Equation (6) reflects the assumption that the peasant class as a whole, always deeply in debt, dissaved as it received credit from the property-owning class (or in good years may have somewhat reduced its debt through the net repayment of outstanding loans).

While the relationships are obviously presented in schematic and simplified form, they do encompass what is essential and will help to clarify the subsequent discussion. I assume implicitly that these relationships and the component elements, especially r and r', remained constant over time (the 1930s and 1940s). As I have already pointed out, this is an approximation which is justified by the relative constancy of agricultural technology and institutional structure over this period. The entire set of income relationships expressed above is meant to provide the backdrop against which the following analysis of the changed conditions brought by the land reform can be most readily understood.

B. Conditions After the Land Reform and Mobilization of the Surplus

$$\Delta Y_p = rQ + r'Q + iL_{tp} = \Delta C_p + \Delta S_p + \Delta M_p \tag{7}$$

$$\Delta M_p = \Delta T_a + \Delta B_a \tag{8}$$

$$T_a = nQ \tag{9}$$

$$B_a = \frac{(P_m - P_z)}{P_z} hQ + \frac{(P_i - P_j)}{P_i} V \tag{10}$$

where: T_a = agricultural taxes;

n = the taxed share of the value of gross agricultural output;

B_a = income extracted from the agricultural sector through government control over the terms of trade with the industrial sector;

P_m = the market price for agricultural products which would be established under competitive conditions;

P_z = the required sales price for agricultural products;

h = required sales as a proportion of the value of
   gross agricultural output;

P_i = the actual price of industrial products;

P_j = the market price for industrial products which
   would be established under competitive conditions;

V = the value of rural purchases of industrial goods.

Equation (7) represents the consequences of the land reform. In the first instance, the income of the property owners ($rQ + r'Q + iL_{tp}$) became incremental peasant income (ΔY_p). Some of this went into added consumption (ΔC_p) (29): this part may be considered a leakage. Some part went into increased peasant saving; but since ΔS_p was not very much larger than S_t, the net effect on national savings was small. (30) Most of the increase in capital formation in the early 1950s was financed through the budget, so that the portion of the peasants' incremental income which the government managed to extract through taxes or manipulation of the terms of trade with the industrial sector, ΔM_p, constituted the main contribution of land reform to raising the national savings level.

Equations (8-10) divide the increased removals from the agricultural sector among increased taxes and public revenue gains from controlling the terms of trade between industry and agriculture. The two elements on the right-hand side of equation (10) represent the gain from depressing the price of agricultural products sold to the industrial sector and the gain from inflating the price of the industrial products sold to the agricultural sector. The choice of P_x and P_i (rather than P_m and P_j) in the denominators reflects the fact that Q and V will be valued in terms of actual prices rather than competitive-market ones. In accordance with the argument presented in Part 1 of this chapter, it was the land reform which made ΔM_p possible. Since the relationships expressed in equations (1-10) illuminate many of the quantitative estimates developed below, I will be referring to them from time to time during the course of the essay.

Two different breakdowns of national income must be incorporated in any effort to relate institutional change of the type under discussion to national saving behavior. To analyze the increase in the national savings ratio requires a partial breakdown of national product by end use, since the only suitable means of estimating this ratio for the post-1950 period is by estimating the investment ratio. At the same time, the direct impact of the land reform was on factor shares, affecting principally property income. The simple model presented below can supplement that above by further clarifying the manner in which changes in property income might affect the share of investment in national expenditure. While it is not always as subject to quantification as the relationships expressed above in equation form, it is more suited to bringing out the change in social relations — and their impact on saving and investment — which the land reform entailed, and to clarifying the implications of alternative strategies for raising the national savings-investment ratio.

As I have noted above, the central task in increasing saving is either to cut consumption (without impairing incentives and therefore output) or to increase output (devoting much of the increase to investment). These alternatives can be clarified in terms of the following scheme of class division (31):
1) owners of property (land and capital);
2) producers of luxury goods and services;
3) producers of subsistence goods and services;
4) producers of capital goods.

The term "producer" encompasses all labor inputs, including management and skilled labor. Land and capital should be treated as productive, but not property ownership per se. (32) This analytic scheme is meant to clarify certain basic production relations, and individuals may be classified in more than one category without destroying its usefulness. The term "subsistence" is meant to apply to those items of consumption which are regarded as everyday necessities by the standards prevailing in a specific country at a specific point in time.

Classes 1, 2, and 4 are maintained by the surplus produced
by class 3 (33) above its own consumption. The output of
class 2 is consumed by class 1. The problem is to increase
the output in class 4. This can be accomplished in one of four
ways:
a. Consumption by one of the other three classes may fall,
making more consumer goods available to finance increased employment in class 4.
b. Real wage rates in class 4 may fall, making possible an
expansion of employment.
c. Productivity in class 4 may rise.
d. The output of subsistence (nonluxury) goods and services
may rise to finance the increase in 4. Alternatively, an
increase in productivity in class 3 with unchanged real
wage rates would release labor and output for transfer to
class 4. (The utilization of underemployed labor would
have the same effect. While the output in 3 may not increase, labor productivity does as fewer workers produce
the same aggregate output. If per capita consumption in
3 remains unchanged, then a surplus appears which may
be used, if it can be extracted from the subsistence sector, to finance an increase in employment and output in 4.)
According to the conventional argument, since it is difficult
to reduce the consumption of any class, an increase in capital
formation requires an increase of subsistence or wage goods
output, an increase in the productivity of this sector, or both. (34)
But to set an increase in output or productivity as the precondition for an underdeveloped country to solve its capital formation
problem also involves difficulties. Technological advance can
increase productivity in 3, but underdeveloped countries commonly find it difficult to make very rapid technological progress,
and what there is must ordinarily be embodied in the form of
new capital equipment. One cannot solve the problem of capital
formation by assuming the availability of capital. For the same
reason, reliance on method "c" is not apt to produce satisfac-
tory results. These considerations do not rule out the possibility

of increasing capital formation via an increase in output but are meant to call attention to the problems involved. (35) On the other hand, the reduction in consumption which the conventional argument dismisses as unrealistic became possibility and ac- tuality in China as a consequence of the land reform.

The central problem here is that of maintaining incentives and output if consumption is reduced. If the return to labor, land, or capital is lowered, it may reduce the services forth- coming from these factors of production. Thus method "b," cutting real wages of employees in the capital goods sector, is unsatisfactory. (36) There is no reason, however, why changes in ownership should affect the input level of capital or land. (37) Moreover, if the new owner's propensity to consume is different from that of the former owner, this change will affect the level of consumption and saving. Consideration of the institutional changes in China in this light provides a useful framework for analysis.

By expropriating the property of those in class 1 via the land reform, the income and therefore the consumption of this class was sharply reduced. (38) At the same time, the demand for the services of those in class 2 disappeared, so that both classes formed a potential pool of increased labor input into classes 3 and 4. This provided a potential source of saving to finance development (the size of this potential source is the sub- ject of Chapter Two). As the task of financing capital formation was then shifted to the government, the question became what part of the saving from the reduction in consumption of classes 1 and 2 could be used to increase employment and output in class 4, and what part would assume some other form.

Among these other forms, which may be considered leakages (from potential saving), three principal categories can be iden- tified:

1. An increase in public services (payments to public ser- vants as a consequence of increased expenditures on edu- cation, public health, the military, etc.).
2. An increase in the per capita consumption of workers in

class 3 with no corresponding increase in employment and output.

3. An increase in the per capita consumption of workers in class 4 with no corresponding increase in employment and output.

Thus the ability of the government to increase the supply of saving depended first on its ability to cut consumption (in class 1 and therefore in class 2 as well) and secondly on its ability to restrict these leakages. To analyze this process, the level of property income in the rural sector and the portion of this associated with the subsequent land reform must first be estimated. This is Y_t $(= rQ + r'Q + iL_{tp})$ in equation (3) above. The second item to be estimated is the level of saving undertaken by those in class 1. This is S_t. The second must be subtracted from the first to determine the consumption of class 1, $C_t + M_t$. (39) The third step to be taken is an estimate of the increase in government revenue, ΔM_p, that can be considered a consequence, direct or indirect, of the land reform. Finally, the share of this which found its way into capital formation can be estimated.

Institutional reform in agriculture did not stop with the land reform. The subsequent process of collectivization, by removing, in large measure, the decision concerning the allocation of income between consumption and saving from the hands of the peasant household and subjecting it to the partial control of public authorities, also had a direct bearing on the financing of capital formation in China. Moreover, consideration of collectivization will help to identify both the lasting consequences and the limitations of land reform's contribution to saving. To complete the picture and to clarify the dynamics of the process as it unfolded in the 1950s, I treat briefly in the final chapter the relationship between collectivization and development finance.

While I deal with the agricultural or rural sector here, the argument concerning the industrial sector is exactly parallel. I have not treated it here because the data are quite fragmentary; because the modern industrial sector was so much smaller than the agricultural sector, accounting for 12% of value added in 1933 as opposed to 65% for the latter (40); and because the more heterogeneous nature of industrial activities makes aggregation of the limited data available highly conjectural.

The strategic and continuing influence of the land reform

Collectivization was consistently the long-run objective of the Chinese Communist Party; never was an agriculture founded on innumerable small independent farm households sought as an end in itself. Land reform, however, was not just a guise to conceal ultimate objectives. Politically, the land reform was meant to crush the power of the gentry-landlord class in rural China and to replace it with that of the poor peasants. Mass participation in the process of confiscation, redistribution, and the meting out of punishment to those who had misused the prerogatives of property and position was an intrinsic part of the process and one which helped to make it irreversible (the previous patterns of authority and subservience could never again be resurrected). At the same time, the distribution of land to more than 60% of the peasantry provided a firm basis of support for the new regime, without which its capacity to rule would have been severely undermined. But undoubtedly, economic considerations played an equal role in the decision to make land reform rather than collectivization the first order of business in transforming the traditional organization of agriculture.

China, lacking the exportable surplus of grain output which prerevolutionary Russia had enjoyed, could not afford the negative impact on production which precipitous and coercive collectivization had had in the USSR. Lacking experienced organizers, managers, and cadres, China, had she followed the Soviet lead, is unlikely to have experienced the rapid recovery in agricultural output which in fact took place in the 1950-1952 period. Perhaps still more important in Chinese thinking was a soundly based application of Marxian economic precepts. According to

Marx, it is the level of development of the productive forces
which determines what relations of production will be appropriate (most productive). With its inability to provide modern
agricultural inputs on a significant scale, the planners argued,
China could find no decisive productivity advantage in collective
organization. Thus the plan for collectivization looked toward
a gradual, step-by-step process which would make possible
acquiring the necessary experience along the way and which
would keep pace with the slowly expanding capacity of industry
to supply tractors, chemical fertilizers, and other modern inputs. I will explain the reasons for abandoning this timetable
and hastening the process in Chapter Four; the point to be
stressed here is that land reform had a clearly defined part to
play in the institutional transformation of agriculture and was
not merely a less-favored substitute adopted because of the
regime's inability to effect its preferred organizational structure.

It may be argued that since the land reform was a transitional
step in a series of institutional changes in agriculture, its impact on consumption and savings behavior could not have been
more than temporary. This view, as I shall show, is not adequate: not only did the sharp increase in the national savings
ratio coincide with the land reform and stem in part from it,
in the manner I have discussed above, but China's ability to
maintain high savings ratios throughout the 1950s was also
connected to the land reform. The rationale for attributing
continuing and strategic influence to the land reform requires
further elaboration.

Only the surplus, that part of national output above prevailing,
socially determined subsistence requirements, will ordinarily
be available for saving, although such income will not necessarily assume this form. The surplus may be divided among
luxury consumption, protection (the maintenance of social order), or investment, as the recipients of this share of national
income choose. The decision depends primarily on the inter-
play of three principal factors: the rate of return on investment

(after taking into account the risks involved); the stability or instability of social life; and prevailing mores with regard to elite consumption (whether one wants to — or is expected to — dress in an elegant fashion, maintain a large house with servants, entertain lavishly, and so forth).

In China before 1949, all three factors tended to minimize the actual saving or investment share: the wealthy found strong attractions to living luxuriously and strong pressures to live reputably, to display their wealth and power; the extreme social disorder meant that the wealthy often had to go beyond collective expenditures on the police and so forth to the bribery of officials and sometimes the maintaining of private gangs (of "running dogs," to use Mao Tse-tung's phrase) to protect their position; and even with such protection social conditions were so unstable as to render most long-term productive investments unreasonably risky. As a consequence, what investment did take place tended to be of an "unproductive" kind — e.g., investment in luxury housing or in inventories, in the latter of which the hoarding of food to take speculative advantage of the regularly recurring famines was of outstanding importance.

In a socialist economy the maximum saving potential can be defined in the same way. Out of a given level of national income, therefore, the higher the prevailing consumption (living) standard, the lower the saving potential. Upward and downward changes in this standard, however, may affect the level of national income itself. An increase in the standard may increase work incentives and, by improving the quality of the labor force, may increase its working capacity and innovative potential. A decrease in the standard will tend to discourage incentives and innovation, and may reduce the very capacity of the labor force to work. (41) Thus, although nominally central planning authorities can determine the level of consumption and investment out of a given level of national income, the existing level of consumption acts as a constraint: efforts to reduce it cannot guarantee an increase in investment as they are apt to reduce national income as well and may also slow future growth by hindering innovative activity. For this reason, the period of land reform or that of transition from capitalism to socialism may assume critical importance. The owners of capital and land may be expropriated without national product falling because ownership per se, as opposed to entrepreneurship or managerial activity, fulfills no productive function. (42) Expropriation releases the surplus, removing the investment decision from the former property owners. A portion of it will go into protection — of the new class in power — typically with a shift in emphasis to meet the external threat posed by hostile capitalist powers. The remainder is divided between an increase in the conventional living standard of the mass of the population and an increase in investment. The transitional period is of essential importance because once prevailing consumption or social subsistence standards have risen, it will be impossible for all practical purposes to reverse the process. In view of these considerations, the division of national income between consumption and investment in the period immediately following the land reform is especially worthy of attention, reflecting the extent to which the Chinese authorities were able to restrict leakages into consumption of the added saving potential which expropriation unleashed.

The impact of land reform upon productivity can be divided into long-run and short-run effects. Typically, short-run effects are apt to be considerable only if the institutional reorganization of agriculture releases unutilized or underutilized resources or inputs for full exploitation. Such may be the case with regard to some of the latifundia in Latin America, for example, where the redistribution of land might, under certain circumstances, result in idle land being brought into production. Such unused inputs of land are not ordinarily present in Asian agriculture, however, and certainly not in the case of China. While it appears that in China, as in other underdeveloped countries, underutilized resources in the form of disguised unemployment existed, the land reform alone was incapable of making this potential input usable. It was not until the collectivization of 1955-1956 and the communization of 1958 that a dramatic increase in labor inputs took place. (43) The increased labor incentive which the elimination of the landlord brought cannot, moreover, have been too great — labor supply curves in the immediate vicinity of subsistence incomes are apt to be more nearly vertical than elsewhere. Thus, as might be expected, in the absence of complementary inputs, improved technology, or an organizational change like collectivization, the short-run impact of land reform on output was small. Although the land reform was consistent with the rapid recovery of agricultural output to prewar peak levels, further improvement was quite limited. (44)

The long-run impact can never really be determined because of the other institutional changes which followed the land reform with a lag of two or three years. Even so, there are ample reasons for thinking that in the absence of modern material inputs embodying new technology and of the consciousness needed to perceive the need for and the manner in which to employ such inputs, land reform in itself could not have dramatically raised agricultural output in China. (45) This, indeed, is one of the principal reasons behind the accelerated transition from the agricultural structure brought about by land reform (small-scale, individual farming) to collectivization. For these reasons, I do not focus in this study on the output-increasing effect of the land reform on the national savings-investment ratio, but on the redistributional effect. Although this involves a "once-and-for-all" change, the redirection of income flows brought about by the land reform and the measures of public policy taken in conjunction with it established a division of national income between consumption and saving (investment) which set the pattern for the 1950s.

Notes

1) See Table 1 in the Statistical Appendix.

2) One mou = approximately one-sixth of an acre.

3) Po Yi-po, "Three Years of Achievements of the People's Republic of China," New China's Economic Achievements 1949-52, comp. China Committee for the Promotion of International Trade (Peking, 1952), pp. 151-52.

4) See Table 1 in the Statistical Appendix.

5) Without economic growth there can be no incremental output capable of being channeled into investment. Insofar as underutilized resources — especially underemployed labor — exist, however, this objection may in part be overcome. But such utilization has nowhere proved possible on a substantial scale without thoroughgoing institutional change. See the discussion of this point in Section 2 of this chapter.

6) This objection leads to the well-known "vicious circle of poverty" thesis, in one form or another.

7) This simply follows because income is a payment for the productive services of the various factors of production and because property (capital and land) accounts for a sizable share of such services.

8) I shall treat the term "luxury consumption" as equivalent to above-average consumption.

9) See the discussion in Chapter Two.

10) This point too is developed in Chapter Two. Note also that land was often purchased by those who had gained wealth elsewhere, but the reverse was uncommon.

11) John L. Buck, Chinese Farm Economy (Chicago, 1930), p. 61.

12) This argument receives its most complete elaboration as a general proposition for the agriculture of underdeveloped countries in Theodore Schultz, Transforming Traditional Agriculture (New Haven, 1964).

13) Such taxes may be difficult and expensive to collect, however. During World War II, the central government took over responsibility for land-tax collection and tightened up tax administration. To collect the tax (in kind) required 200,000 men working in a separate organization within the Ministry of

Finance. Arthur N. Young, China's Wartime Finance and Inflation 1937-1945 (Cambridge, Mass., 1965), p. 24.

14) Buck, in a letter to Arthur Young, estimated that perhaps one-third of China's arable land was unregistered and therefore off the tax rolls. Ibid., p. 22.

15) The tenor of the times is reflected in the final declaration of a conference convened under the auspices of the Ministry of Finance in May 1934. It stated, in part: "The rampancy of banditry, illegal taxation and extravagance, bringing with them additional burdens to the people, have resulted in rural bankruptcy.... The Conference has adopted a total of over 100 resolutions, the most important of which are...1. Reduction of farm taxation in order to alleviate the sufferings of the farmers.... The Government will be petitioned to issue a mandate perpetually forbidding the increase of the farm dues.... The existing surtaxes...should be gradually reduced with a view to their total abolition." The China Year Book 1936 (Shanghai, 1936), pp. 384-85.

16) This is not the only explanation for economic growth in Taiwan: note too Japanese development of the island's infrastructure, especially in agriculture and particularly in irrigation, United States' foreign aid, and the modest land reform.

17) Audrey Donnithorne, China's Economic System (London, 1967), pp. 40-41.

18) Most typically, this was financed by the mortgaging of land to finance emergency or ceremonial expenses. The high interest on the loans secured frequently precluded repayment, so that the mortgaging of land was often the first step in losing it. This process, together with the resulting concentration of land ownership and growth of absentee ownership, is described by R. H. Tawney, Land and Labour in China, pp. 67-68, Chen Han-seng, Landlord and Peasant in China, pp. 95-96, and Fei Hsiao-tung, Peasant Life in China, pp. 183-84 and 191, and Earthbound China, pp. 201, 205-6, and 292-96.

19) See the excellent discussion by C. K. Yang in The Chinese Family in the Communist Revolution, reprinted in Chinese

Communist Society: The Family and the Village (Cambridge, Mass., 1965), chap. 2.

20) Ceremonial expenses sometimes provided a redistributional element, as when the rich invited poor relations to their feasts. In addition, festive occasions made a general contribution to welfare by brightening village life. Despite these qualifications, however, the chief function of these occasions was conspicuous consumption and the promotion of security, and the dissaving associated with them drained off substantial funds that might have been devoted to investment purposes.

21) Paul Baran, whose Political Economy of Growth (New York, 1962) was one of the first works to analyze extensively the role of the surplus in economic development, defines surplus in three different ways: actual economic surplus is the difference between society's actual current output and its actual current consumption (p. 22); potential economic surplus is the difference between the potential output of society if all factors of production are fully and efficiently utilized and essential consumption (p. 23); and planned economic surplus is the difference between "optimal" (planned) output and "optimal" (planned) consumption (pp. 41-42). While the concept of potential surplus comes closest to my usage of the term here, none of the three fits it exactly.

22) See Note 54 in Chapter Two for the results of one survey of landlord occupations in Kiangsu Province.

23) The National Income of Communist China (New York, 1961), p. 3.

24) At the same time, it is necessary to distinguish between saving in the agricultural sector per sé and the extent to which the land reform can be said to be responsible for making such saving possible. These are differentiated in the discussion of Chapter Three, while Section 3 in this chapter elaborates the rationale behind focusing on the role of the land reform.

25) The Economy of the Chinese Mainland: National Income and Economic Development 1933-1959 (Princeton, 1965), p. 140. This work, carried out with modern national-income-

accounting methods, is the most comprehensive study of China's national income. Since, moreover, the period covered coincides with that under review here, the Liu and Yeh estimates will be cited often.

26) See Charles F. Remer, Foreign Investments in China (New York, 1933), for estimates of the size of these remittances in the early 1930s.

27) According to John L. Buck, only about one-quarter of farm credit was for productive purposes. Land Utilization in China (New York, 1968), p. 461.

28) If hoarding takes the form of holding money, it does not use up real resources, which may therefore be available for investment. If, however, hoarding takes the form of investment in stocks of goods, it does use real resources, diverting them from potentially more productive uses. Luxury housing is an investment only when new housing is built. In general, by "non-productive" investments I mean those that do not contribute directly to the expansion of production in subsequent periods.

29) Besides the increase in per capita consumption, the size of the peasantry grew with the influx of former landlords.

30) The land reform did bring some increase in self-investment in agriculture. See the discussion of the magnitudes involved in Chapter Three.

31) I am indebted here to the stimulus provided by the similar model which W. Arthur Lewis culled from the classics and which appeared in his article, "Unlimited Labour: Further Notes," The Manchester School, XXVI (January 1958), 1-32. Lewis, however, distinguishes services and luxuries from wage goods, treating, in effect, all services as luxuries. I think it more meaningful to distinguish between luxury goods and services, on the one hand, and subsistence goods and services (necessities) on the other.

32) The argument is neatly put by Joan Robinson in An Essay on Marxian Economics (London, 1963), pp. 17-19.

33) Working, like other producing groups, with the aid of land and capital.

34) This argument is presented by W. Arthur Lewis, op. cit., among others. Moreover, the whole thrust of schemes to increase capital formation through utilizing underemployed labor, such as that Nurkse presents in Problems of Capital Formation in Underdeveloped Countries (New York, 1964), suggests that they constitute a deus ex machina meant to circumvent the difficulty of reducing consumption in poor countries. This difficulty, however, is not so severe as it may at first appear: see my argument in the text for an explanation.

35) This is the strategy which most countries seeking to develop without disturbing the position of vested interests have had to use. Oil-rich countries especially (e.g., Iran) have frequently been able to follow this course with some measure of success.

36) Such a measure would have been unreasonable in any event in the Chinese context, with real wages typically at a subsistence level to start with.

37) Assuming that rational economic behavior is maintained. If the change in ownership comes via expropriation, there may be a temporary decline in incentives to add to the capital stock. This is a problem of the transitional period, whose significance depends upon the skill with which the changeover is handled and the extent to which those expropriated had been undertaking investment.

38) The reduction in consumption of those in class 1 does not mean that the individuals involved were left with no source of income: it means that they received no income qua property owners. While some ex-landlords, accused of crimes, were executed by aroused villagers and others fled the country, typically, and as prescribed by the Land Reform Law, former landlords were allocated an amount of land to farm themselves equal to the average per capita holding in the locality.

39) Landowner tax payments, M_t, can be treated most reasonably as part of the collective consumption of the property-owning class: net public investment was negligible in the 1930s, and there can be little question about the strong class-interest

bias of both local and national government.

40) Liu and Yeh, The Economy of the Chinese Mainland, p. 89.

41) Or, as happened in Poland in December 1970, efforts to reduce consumption may provoke so much social unrest as to be unsustainable.

42) If entrepreneurship and management are intertwined with ownership, the prevention of output falling when expropriation takes place depends on their successful separation.

43) See Table 9 in the Statistical Appendix.

44) See Table 4-1 in Chapter Four for the output data.

45) See the discussion in Doreen Warriner, Land Reform in Principle and Practice (Oxford, 1969), chap. 2, "The Effect on Production."

CHAPTER TWO

The property share in the rural sector

The reality is always more complex than the models which may be employed in attempting to render it coherent. The fabric of modern Chinese history especially, rich and variegated in texture, cannot be smoothed and stretched to comply with the requirements of any preconceived model without doing some violence to the underlying reality. I have taken two principal measures to mitigate this problem. First, I have tried to incorporate in the text a substantial amount of descriptive material, much of it in the form of quotes from the original sources, to accompany the data. Acquainting the reader with some of the source materials directly can also help, moreover, to form the basis for independent calculations. There is some room for difference of opinion concerning a number of the estimates presented in this chapter (the Appendix shows how variations in the assumptions will affect the estimates), although I hope I shall be able to convince the reader of the reasonableness of most of them. The analytic framework which I use, however, is perfectly general and perfectly consistent, so that the reader will find that he can substitute his own assumptions if he so chooses and still make use of the framework provided. It is with the multiple purpose of revealing the historical ambiguities involved, persuading the reader of the correctness of my assumptions, and providing him with a basis for dissent should he choose to go his own way that I have quoted extensively from the source materials.

Second, I have tried to organize the discussion in such a way
that the limitations of the equations and class model I have
used, limitations which any attempt to simplify and systema-
tize historical reality — economic or otherwise — must involve,
do not become a hindrance to understanding. The reader can
best grasp the rationale for the flexibility involved by keeping
in mind that this chapter is meant to uncover some of the principal income flows in the traditional economy of China, income
flows whose subsequent redirection through the process of revolution and reform made some part of the following increase in
saving and investment possible. It is for this reason, for example, that I am concerned with nominal factor shares (e.g.,
actual rent receipts) rather than with analytical factor shares
(e.g., including imputed rents): as it was the land rented out to
others which was, in the main, subject to redistribution, rather
than the land of owner-farmers, it was the actual rental income
of landlords which was affected by the land reform and not the
imputed rental income of average peasant proprietors. Moreover, and of equal importance, is the fact that the traditional
economy formed a coherent system, only certain parts of which
can be grasped by any abstract economic model. Out of the
landlord's gross income, for example, he may have allocated
funds to hire a rent collector and several aides, often charac-
ters of dubious reputation (1), to safeguard his property and
insure that all money owed to him was paid. Much of the function of local government, which he supported with taxes and
contributions, was to assure him that his property rights would
be maintained. (2) The income of his personal employees and
that of the local government employees, even though the social
role of these people was to perpetuate a system in which the
rights of property would be maintained, in formal terms served
to swell the labor share of national income and to diminish the
property share. By transforming the entire system, the revolution and land reform affected all of these income flow requirements and patterns, not just those of the landlord himself. To
draw the picture in its entirety, then, some flexibility in treating

material which may appear to go beyond the formal requirements of a discussion of the property share may be necessary;
and I have, accordingly, permitted myself to transgress in just
such a fashion, especially toward the close of the chapter.

While this material should not be treated with excessive
rigidity, sight should not be lost of the rationale for using an
approach which is concerned with factor shares. First of all,
any model will have such limitations, and most much more,
but models are nevertheless useful as a means of organizing
information. More important, it is the income flows to owners
of property which stood at the center of the traditional Chinese
system I have been discussing and the revolution which transformed it. This point will best be clarified by the discussion
of this chapter itself. Finally, the very sterility of land-rent
payments and other returns to the owners of property in the
rural sector, a consequence of the unwillingness of the landowners of China to devote a significant share of their income
to productive investment (3), is precisely what makes this income category important. With the opportunity cost of diverting
the income which flowed to this group close to zero (from the
standpoint of saving and investment), this flow constituted a
major potential source of untapped development finance. In
England the large landowners took the lead in bringing about
the eighteenth century agricultural revolution which paved the
way for the industrial revolution. In Japan the early Meiji
landlords, often farmers themselves, took the lead in introduc-
ing scientific agriculture into their localities and invested
vigorously in agriculture and associated commercial and industrial enterprises. Impinging on the property share in England or Japan would probably have retarded economic growth.
In China it could only have the opposite effect. (4)

The disposal of the surplus by the landlords is, as I have
indicated, less amenable to statistical analysis than the ori-
gins of their income. The problems are complicated not only
by a lack of aggregate data but by the differences among landlords themselves. Landlords might be residents of the rural

locality, of a market town, or of a larger city. In general, it
appears that the larger the extent of a landowner's holdings,
the more apt he was to be an urban resident; it also appears
that the proportion of land held by absentee landowners was
greater the closer the land was to a large city. How the landowners used their income depended, of course, on their living
circumstances, and those living in urban areas had a much
wider choice than their rural counterparts.

Despite the difficulties of aggregation, a number of pre-
Liberation village studies provide considerable insight into the
expenditure patterns of landowners and rich peasants and the
contrast between their luxury (above-average) consumption and
the living standards of the poor and landless peasants. Since
the most fundamental consequence of the land reform was to
transform the surplus from luxury consumption into investment
and subsistence consumption, consideration of some of these
studies may help to illuminate the opportunity costs and benefits of the land reform.

Fei Hsiao-tung describes the living pattern of the landlords
in Yuts'un, Yunnan Province, in the following manner. (5) The
home of a typical wealthy (landowner) villager would consist of
ten rooms (contrasted to the typical one room of the poor and landless peasants) and extensive furnishings and decorations. The best
house in the village was owned by a man called the "Fifth Lord."

His house, which was entered by a large carved gate, leading into a courtyard in which flowers and trees were growing, consisted of at least forty rooms, built around five
connecting courtyards, each with its gardens. The rooms
were large and well furnished; there were carved wooden
window frames and glass in the windows, painted and deco-
rated beams, and in certain of the rooms not only Western-
type decorations but a Western-style sofa. . . .

The "lord" wears long silk gowns, which are soft and
light. He need not walk, because he has a ricksha. He keeps
a cow to give milk; takes ginseng root and the tip of a deer's

horn, which give vitality; and smokes opium. The women in
the house dress in long robes made of silk or fine cotton
materials. The young men wear foreign-style student uni-
forms. Besides their regular meals, they have an extra one
at midnight; and in a year they consume 650 pounds of meat
as well as several dozen chickens and ducks. When the
family wish to, they go to Kunming, simply for diversion.
In a year they spend about $20,000. This is the outstandingly
wealthy home in the village. (6)

While this landlord was undoubtedly more wealthy than the
typical landlord, the pattern of his expenditure reveals the basic
categories of luxury consumption that landowners and rich
peasants could enjoy. The large house, its maintenance, land-
scaping, and furnishing were major outlets for luxury expenditure, as was a food-consumption standard far above prevailing
norms. Expenditures on clothing that far surpassed in quantity
and quality what the typical peasant could buy were also char-
acteristic. The keeping of a rickshaw meant the need for a
laborer to pull it. Personal services were also supplied this
family by its maidservants; the cost for this was only their
room, board, and presumably some clothing, however, as they
were given no salary.

Luxury expenditure is also reflected in this family in its
consumption of medicines and drugs: ginseng, deer's horn, and
opium are all costly items. This family could also travel simply for diversion and educate its sons. (7) Not mentioned explicitly here, but an important outlet for luxury consumption
nevertheless, were expenditures on jewelry, artwork, and so
forth. In brief, then, the rural surplus in China typically took
the form of luxury expenditure on housing, furnishings, food,
clothing, jewelry, artwork, personal services, medicines and
drugs, education, and travel and entertainment. Our understanding of these consumption patterns may be deepened by considering the difference between the rich and the poor and landless peasants in Luts'un, a village also in Yunnan Province.

There the wealth of the rich peasants is less remarkable, but
the difference between them and the poor is no less striking.

Households A and B represent the landowning class.... Although neither of these households is considered to be the
wealthiest in the village, the standards of living of both are
representative of the upper stratum. Each owns a two-story
house with three rooms on the ground floor and a large porch
extending the length of the front wall. The porch is the locus
for eating and most other domestic activities, while a central
room, containing the best furniture and the ancestral tablets,
is reserved for more formal occasions. The remaining two
rooms are partitioned to make three or four sleeping com-
partments....

The members of households A and B wear excellent clothing. The heads of the families have long robes for formal
occasions, as well as hip-length jackets for ordinary wear,
some made of silk or other expensive materials. The wom-
en likewise are provided with good wardrobes, which include
silver earrings and hair ornaments. In household A the boy
wore a student uniform with leather shoes and European
shirts, and the three-year-old child wore knitted jackets
and caps of foreign style.... These families also maintain
a high standard for the food they consume....

Households D and E are representative of the landless
families. They do not own their own homes but rent ram-
shackle, one-room huts outside the gates of the village.
While we were visiting household E one day, following a
period of rainy weather, part of the saturated earth walls of
the dark, windowless house suddenly collapsed, letting in a
flood of unaccustomed light. We were appalled by this catastrophe; but the family accepted it calmly, for, as we learned,
it was a frequent occurrence. The wife simply remarked
that once more they would have a poor night's sleep. Then
we discovered that the water was still trickling through the
poor thatching of the roof into the attic where the family

slept. The building in which Household D lived was equally
unsatisfactory.... Both houses are almost constantly filled
with smoke, since, by reason of the inadequate clothing of
the occupants, a fire is essential for warmth in chilly weather and since poverty necessitates the burning of grass and
wood rather than charcoal. The smoke was so heavy that
we... were unable to open our eyes.... Inasmuch as the
activities of almost all the occupants are carried on within
the walls of these wet, smoky hovels, it is not surprising
that, although each family had produced six or seven children, only one was alive at the time we were in the village....
The living members all suffer from trachoma, and the head
of Household D is nearly blind. Both of these families depend entirely upon wages for their livelihood. (8)

In this village, the poorer people ate only two meals a day
except when working on the farm, while the more prosperous
were distinguished by always eating three meals a day. While
the opulence of the more well-to-do families was by no means
comparable to that of the wealthiest family in Yuts'un, the pattern of luxury consumption was basically similar. Luxury
items entering into the consumption of the families in Luts'un
included housing, furnishings, clothing, jewelry, food, education,
entertainment, and medicine. The poor families, by contrast,
spent practically nothing on items other than food, clothing, and
housing (and taxes), yet still could not reach a subsistence level
of living.

The foregoing descriptions have focused on the daily-life expenditures. In addition to these, the expenses for elaborate
ceremonies at the time of marriage, death, and other occasions
accounted for a substantial share of the surplus. Even with this
inclusion, however, the description of the rural surplus is not
complete. Throughout rural China it was common to find the
surplus manifested not in luxury consumption but in abstinence
from labor.

In Luts'un, approximately 30% of the landowners, both the

rich peasants and those renting out land, were able to free
themselves from physical labor. If they had been prepared to
make the same work effort as others, their incomes would have
been much higher still, and this in turn would have been reflected in higher levels of luxury consumption. Instead, however, they preferred to refrain from working once their incomes were moderately higher than subsistence requirements.
In such cases the surplus is expressed in the form of potential
surplus, the income foregone by not working, as well as in the
form of nonessential consumption expenditure.

Another example of the importance of leisure in rural social
life is provided by Tadashi Fukutake's description of a village
near Suchow in central China.

> Except during the busy season, the upper and upper-middle
> class farmers go marketing in town every morning. It is
> the man's job, not his wife's; on the way home from the
> market — vegetables, meat, and fish in hand — they drop
> in the teahouse to chat and exchange news. The wealthy go
> to town again in the afternoon to rest at the teahouse, some-
> times to play mahjong. The teahouse in Fengchiao is a place
> where prominent villagers can meet townspeople and leaders
> from other villages. (9)

According to the earlier discussion, whether the surplus takes
an actual or potential form, reflected in the luxury consumption
or abstinence from labor that the ownership of property makes
possible, will not substantially affect the analysis here. The
property income flows in the rural sector sustained both forms
of the surplus, and by focusing on these flows we need not be
concerned with making a precise quantitative estimate of the
relative importance of the two forms. This is fortunate because although we know that both forms were significant, we
do not have sufficient data to estimate the relative magnitudes.
The property share, by contrast, we can estimate; and it was
the return to the owners of property that gave them the option

of enjoying luxury goods or leisure.

Estimation of the property share in the rural sector requires that it be broken down into its various components: land rent, farm business profits, interest income, and commercial profits. Each of these except commercial profits will be treated separately below. Retail trade in rural areas was carried on largely by peddlers, and there is no convenient way to distinguish between the profit and wage components of the value added ascribed to them. Moreover, and of greater concern, none of the national income studies appear to include in their trade categories the (overlapping) occupations of speculator, agricultural middleman, and wholesale merchant, perhaps because aggregative data on these groups are simply unavailable. This omission is particularly serious if we take note of the fact that nearly two-thirds of marketed farm products were sold through middlemen (10) and that several local studies have indicated that more than a quarter of the goods consumed by agricultural families were purchased. (11) Since the nature of the business activities of middlemen is extremely heterogeneous, varying also over time and from region to region, it is perhaps impossible to systematically aggregate and extrapolate the scattered cases of which we have knowledge. It is only possible to note then that while wholesaler profits may well have been considerable (12), there is no reasonable basis for estimating their aggregate level.

I am using the term "property" to include land as well as capital, since changes in the ownership of land should have no more effect on the productive services which it affords than changes in the ownership of reproducible capital. Thus the institutional changes which affected land ownership can be treated in the same general framework, which has been elaborated in Chapter One, as institutional changes which affected the other components of the property share in the rural sector. Since land rent is the single most important component in the rural sector, it is to this that I shall turn first.

Land rent

To assess the potential contribution of land reform to capital formation, the magnitude of prereform land rents must first be determined. Three considerations make this task less imposing than might appear at first sight. First, only rents which took the form of actual payments in cash or kind by one party to another need be estimated: imputed rents may be omitted. This is because, with only one significant exception, the land managed directly by rich peasants using hired labor (which will be treated separately under the category "farm business profits" below), it was the redirection of the actual rental payments which contributed, according to the schema outlined in Chapter One, to the post-land-reform increase in saving in the agricultural sector. Second, in most cases percentages and ratios rather than absolute figures will be sufficient, as the following discussion will show. Third, as was stressed in Chapter One, while the data limitations preclude obtaining the exact figures involved, knowledge of even the correct orders of magnitude can make a significant contribution to understanding the course and consequences of institutional change in China.

The form in which land rent will be considered, then, is in terms of its share, and especially that of explicit land rent, in the national income or net domestic product. While the base year is still 1933, much of the data are for years scattered on either side of 1933: with the amount of information available limited, such data cannot be neglected. Moreover, the relative constancy of agricultural techniques and conditions in the "traditional" economy and the absence of any pronounced trend in aggregate agricultural output in the entire period under consideration lend validity to this procedure.

The share of rent received by landlords in national income can be estimated by multiplying together three ratios: the share of rent in value added on rented land (R/Y_{ar}); the proportion of net value added in agriculture which is added on rented land (Y_{ar}/Y_a); and the share of value added in agriculture in total value added in the economy (Y_a/Y), where R represents rent payments, Y_{ar} is the value added on rented land, Y_a is the value added in agriculture, and Y is the total value added in the economy. The product of the three ratios (R/Y) is the rent received by landlords as a proportion of total value added in the economy: rent as a proportion of national income. This relationship may be represented as follows:

$$\frac{R}{Y_{ar}} \times \frac{Y_{ar}}{Y_a} \times \frac{Y_a}{Y} = \frac{R}{Y}$$

For the third ratio, the share of value added in agriculture in total value added in the economy, the 65% estimate of Liu and Yeh is soundly based. (13) For the first ratio, the share of rent in value added on rented land, fairly considerable variation is to be found in different regions in the country, with most of the data indicating the share of total receipts or the share of the main crop paid the landlord, rather than the share of value added. Even so, this information is useful in estimating the ratio in question. Table 2-1 summarizes the information available.

Table 2-1

Rent Paid as Percent of Output

Reference and Place	Year	Amount (%)	Basis (as reported)
1) North and East China	early 1920s	24.6-66.6 average 40.5	total (gross) receipts
2) Szechwan	1941	71 32	main crop gross receipts
3) Hunan	about 1935	50	total crop
4) Wei-hsien, Shantung	1930s	50 (nominal) 56-70 (after extra charges)	main crop main crop

Table 2-1 (continued)

Reference and Place	Year	Amount (%)	Basis (as reported)
4) Wuhu, Anhwei		50	crop
4) Paotow	1920s	50	crop
		30 (after famine and increase in banditry)	crop
4) Kashing (lower Yangtse)		23.92	total expenses
5) Chekiang	1928	45 (not including rent deposit, presents to landlord, and transport fees)	total expenses produce
6) Hupeh (parts of)		50	produce
6) Kiangsu (parts of)		55	produce
6) Hunan (parts of)		50-60	produce
6) Kwangtung (small farms)		55-66	produce
7) Luts'un, Yunnan	1939-1943	60 (nominal)	main crop (rice)
		33-60 (actual)	
7) Yits'un, Yunnan	1939-1943	50	the product
7) Yuts'un, Yunnan	1939-1943	50 (tenant assumes risk and provides all tools and capital)	rice
8) Ting-hsien, Hopei	1928-1931	50 (share rent)	the crop
		35-40 (fixed cash rent)	average gross income

Table 2-1 (continued)

Reference and Place	Year	Amount (%)	Basis (as reported)
9) Kwangtung:	early-mid 1930s		
Tai-shan		50 (paid by 70% of tenants)	crop
Southwest Kwangtung		more than 50	crop
Lien-kiang		65	total harvest
Pan-yu		55	harvest
Eastern Kwang-tung		50	harvest
Pearl River Delta (part)		as high as 70-90	main crop
Kwangtung (all)		50-57	entire harvest
10) Nanching, Pearl River Delta	1940s	43-50 plus rent deposit on high- and medium-grade land; 25% plus rent deposit on low-grade land	entire yield
11) all China, rice farming, average	1920s-30s	44.9-51.5	output
11) all China, dry farming, average	1920s-30s	43.6-47.8	output
12) all China, rice farming, average	1920s-30s	42.49-44.07	output
12) all China, dry farming, average	1920s-30s	42.57-46.44	output
13) Kunyang, Yunnan	1930s-40s	at least 50% (sometimes less for in-fertile land)	produce

Table 2-1 (continued)

Reference and Place	Year	Amount (%)	Basis (as reported)
14) Chang-teh hsien, Honan	1939	50-80	main crop or total output, depending on extent to which landlord provided production inputs
15) Tai-an hsien, Shantung	1939	50	main crop, plus 0-100% of subsidiary crops, depending on landlord's provision of production inputs
16) Kaihsienkung, Kiangsu	1930s	40	total rice output

Sources:

1. John L. Buck, Chinese Farm Economy, p. 149.

2. Buck, Agricultural Survey of Szechuan Province, China, p. 2.

3. China, Bureau of Foreign Trade, Hunan, An Economic Survey, p. 8.

4. Agrarian China, pp. 17, 31, 44, 78-79.

5. The China Year Book 1934, p. 767.

6. R. H. Tawney, Land and Labour in China, p. 66.

7. Fei Hsiao-tung and Chang Chih-I, Earthbound China: A Study of Rural Economy in Yunnan, pp. 75, 154, 157, 224.

8. Sidney D. Gamble, Ting Hsien: A North China Rural Community, p. 215.

9. Chen Han-seng, Landlord and Peasant in China, pp. ix, 22, 60-62.

10. C. K. Yang, A Chinese Village in Early Communist Transition, p. 49.

11. Materials on China's Modern Agricultural History, Vol. III, 1927-1937, pp. 247-248 (in Chinese).

12. Selected Statistical Materials on China's Modern Economic History, p. 303 (in Chinese).

13. Hsiao-tung Fei and Yung-teh Chow, China's Gentry, p. 273.

14. South Manchurian Railway, Research Division, Report on the Agricultural Situation in North China: Chang-teh Hsien, Honan, pp. 69-73 (in Japanese).

15. South Manchurian Railway, North China Economic Research Institute, Report on the Agricultural Situation in North China: Tai-an Hsien, Shantung, p. 30 (in Japanese).

16. Fei Hsiao-tung, Peasant Life in China: A Field Study of Country Life in the Yangtze Valley, p. 188.

As I will show in the more detailed discussion of these data on the following pages, the evidence suggests that the tenant paid, on balance, 35-45% of his gross output value as rent, with 40% the most reasonable estimate and the lower and upper extremes of this range serving as low and high estimates, respectively. The studies on which these estimates are based vary widely in coverage and methodology, and some discussion of them will be necessary to put these figures in their proper perspective. This discussion will also contribute to clarifying the basis for the subsequent adjustments in the 40% figure — the share of rent in the gross value of agricultural output on rented land — which will be required to obtain the share of rent in value added on rented land. First, however, some mention of rental systems and other tenure arrangements will help to clarify the picture.

For China as a whole, some 22% of the tenants paid their rent according to a share-rent system, 25% according to a cash-rent system, 51% according to a cash-crop system, and 2% according to a cropper system. (14) Under the share-rent system the risk was divided between tenant and landlord, each receiving a certain proportion of the crop. Under the cash system the tenant agreed to pay a fixed amount of cash as rent; and under the cash-crop system the tenant agreed to pay a fixed amount of the crop or its monetary equivalent. Such "fixed" payments, however, did reflect land productivity and were often adjusted according to the size of the harvest the previous year, so that while the landowner was partially relieved from sharing the risk which the share-rent system entailed, the possibility of the tenant realizing windfall gains or benefitting from his own improvements was sharply limited. Under the cropper system, the tenant's return was very small, as he provided only the labor while the landlord provided all the working capital as well as the fixed capital. In general, however, the tenant was responsible for the management of the farm and the provision of working capital.

In a 1921-1924 study covering 486 farms in five provinces, John L. Buck found the following averages for tenant- and landlord-provided capital per rented farm (in Chinese dollars or yuan):

Table 2-2

Provision of Capital in Rented Farms
by Tenant and Landlord

	Tenant	Landlord
Land	Ch. $ 2.36	Ch. $1,465.5
Buildings	107	131.4
Livestock	63	23
Trees	16	11
Supplies (seeds, fertilizer, etc.)	36	0.6
Farm equipment	43.5	2.3
Total	$268	$1,634

Source: John L. Buck, Chinese Farm Economy, p. 61.

Hiring human or animal labor, common even on rented farms during the busy seasons, was an expense typically borne completely by the tenants.

In a wider sample from the same study, Buck found that in eleven localities in north and east central China in the early 1920s, the share of total receipts taken by the landlord ranged from 24.6 to 66.6%, averaging 40.5%. (15) In Szechwan Province, according to an investigation carried out by Buck and the Farmer's Bank of China in 1941, the average rental was 71% of the main crop, rice (16), which rental represented 31.8% of gross receipts. (17) Further, Buck noted that:

> The proportion of farm cash and non-cash expenses for both owners and tenants, when interest on investment in land and buildings is charged owners, is 40% for labor (hired and family labor, including board, but excluding the operator's labor); 43% for use of land and 17% for seed, feed, fertilizer, implements and livestock purchased during the year. (18)

For the province of Hunan as a whole, a national government survey of the province revealed that tenants paid about 50% of their total crop as land rent. (19) It should be noted too that in many parts of China there was a distinction between actual and nominal rent payments. Besides the widespread instances of outright dishonesty (20), the tenant was subject to a variety of special exactions. In Wei-hsien, Shantung, for example:

> In the collection of such a share rent, the nominal share differs from the real share. Nominally the tenant keeps half the grain crop and all the residue together with any grass-like catch crop grown especially for fuel. In reality, however, a considerable portion of the crop... is taken by the landlord before the 50-50 division is made... as a supposed compensation for his not getting any of the residue or catch crop... [additional amounts would] go to the village chief or rent-collecting agent. These are apportioned to

him on the theory that he must be compensated for all his labor and expenditure in connection with the collecting... care of the threshing floor and the transporting of grain to the granary.

Just how much of the crop is taken away under these names varies in different places, but in the western part of Wei-hsien the big landlords have established a standard total amount as follows: for wheat 12% of the harvest; for kaoliang 26 to 30%; for millet 30 to 40%, and for various kinds of beans 12 to 13%. According to this scale, the tenant therefore can only keep 44% of his wheat or bean crop, 35 to 37% of his kaoliang, and 30 to 35% of his millet. (21)

Near Wuhu in southern Anhwei, the tenants furnished their own seed, fertilizer, and fodder and paid about half their crop as rent. (22) In Paotow, the proportion paid as rent fell to about 30% from 50% following an increase in banditry and famine which reduced the number of tenants. (23) In Kashing, midway between Hangchow and Shanghai in the lower Yangtze region, wages (including imputed wages) made up 22.26% of total expenses and rent 23.92%, with 6.91% going for taxes and the remainder for the farmhouse, livestock, agricultural implements, seeds, fertilizer, and other inputs. (24)

The above estimates do not include the unpaid labor service which the tenant was obliged, in many regions, to give the landlord on special occasions. Other exactions too may not be indicated fully. The situation in Chekiang Province was reported in The China Year Book 1934 as follows:

Professor Franklin Ho, a very prudent economist, estimates in a study made in Chekiang for the Institute of Research in Social Science in 1928 (since when rents have been steadily rising) that the farmer paid 45% of his produce to the landlord. It is the custom in some provinces to pay only according to the basic crops produced, but in others the share is calculated out of the total produce of the farm, both bye and

main products. This figure should be increased since it
does not include deposits paid by the tenants (and not as a
rule recovered), presents which it is customary to make to
the landlord, and payments for the transportation (sometimes
amounting to an extra 8% on the rent) of the produce to the
landlord's farm or agency. (25)

R. H. Tawney describes the results of a sample study reported by C. C. Chang (26) which indicates "the percentage of
the yield taken by the landlord under (i) the share-rent system,
by which he shares the risk with the tenant and receives a fixed
proportion of the crop, whatever the latter may be, and (ii) the
crop-rent system, by which he receives a payment in kind
stipulated in advance":

Table 2-3

Share of the Yield Going to the Landlord

Land Quality	Superior	Medium	Inferior
(i) Share rent	%	%	%
irrigated land	52	48	45
nonirrigated land	48	45	44
(ii) Crop rent			
irrigated land	46.3	46.2	45.8
nonirrigated land	45.3	44.6	44.4

Source: C. C. Chang, "Farm Tenancy in China," China Critic,
September 30, 1930; reported in Tawney, Land and Labour in
China, p. 66.

The 1930s was a period of considerable social ferment in
China and one in which there was a great deal of interest in and
receptivity to various facets of Western culture. This included
the empirically oriented social science research methods developed abroad and was reflected in frequent local surveys of

social and especially economic conditions of the sort just described. Two exceptionally able investigators in this sphere
were Fei Hsiao-tung and Chen Han-seng, both of whose works
I have referred to above; their data on the rental share also
merit individual attention. In Earthbound China: A Study of
Rural Economy in Yunnan, Fei, together with Chang Chih-I,
describes the results of the field investigation of three Yunnan
villages (southwestern China) undertaken during the period
1939-1943. In one of the three, Luts'un, the nominal rental was
60% of the rice crop, although that high a rate was rarely found
in practice: the authors cite instances where the payment was
50%, 33%, and 55% of the crop and only one case where it
reached 60% (as a consequence of a rise in the rental fee following a good harvest the previous year). (27) In another village, Yits'un, mention is made of one-half the product going to
the owner as rent (which left the tenant with less than he could
earn at the going wages for agricultural labor). (28) In the
third village, Yuts'un, the average rent was also one-half the
rice produced, with the tenant providing all the tools and capital. (29)

Chen Han-seng, aided by a team of investigators, carried out
extensive rural surveys throughout Kwangtung Province in the
early and middle 1930s. He describes the situation in different
parts of the province as follows:

> In Tai-shan, 70 per cent of the tenants pay a fixed rent in
> grain, which is about 50 per cent of the crop. In the districts of
> North River Valley, such as Loh-chang and Kuh-kiang, the
> amount is considerably less. In the southwestern part of
> the province it is often much more. Hoh-pu is a good ex-
> ample; the fixed rent in grain predominates there. In a few
> cases the rent is paid once a year after the harvest of the
> second crop but it is paid usually twice a year: 40 per cent
> after the first crop and 60 per cent after the second. This
> fixed rent is at least 30 per cent of the crop, but in a great major-
> ity of cases it is as much as 60 per cent. In the vicinity of Chang-

huang, in the northern part of Hoh-pu, where the hilly lands
are not rocky but very fertile, a higher productivity has
created a higher rent. For, after paying 60 per cent of
grain as a fixed rent, the tenant here still makes regular
presents to his landlord. The fixed rent in grain in Lien-
kiang, a district immediately east of Hoh-pu, is usually
65 per cent of the total harvest. It is not unusual, therefore, to
hear of tenants in Lien-kiang who sell their children in order to pay the rent. Boys or girls of ten years of age are
being sold for less than 100 yuan per capita....

A part of Pan-yu also has fixed rent in grain; its amount
is ordinarily 55 per cent of the harvest and rarely exceeds
60 per cent. In the districts of Lien-hsien, Ju-yuen, Jen-
hwa, and Wung-yuen, all located in North River Valley, the
amount of fixed rent in grain is somewhat smaller, usually
40 per cent of the harvest. Only in a few places of Ying-
teh and Nan-hsiung does it amount to 50 per cent. With the
exceptions of Fung-shun, where it is 30 per cent of the produce, of Chiao-ling, where it is 45 per cent, and of Hsing-
ning and Wu-hwa, where it is 40 per cent, the eastern portion of Kwangtung, generally speaking, has a fixed rent in
grain, amounting to one-half the harvest. In the valley of
West River, generally speaking, such a rent is from 40 to
60 per cent. The proportion of rent paid in grain is largest
in relation to the harvest, as we have seen above, in the
districts of southwestern Kwangtung. (30)

Rentals ran even higher than those cited above for the exceptionally rich farmland of the Pearl River Delta region,
which constitutes about 2,500,000 mou, or one-sixteenth of all
the cultivated land in the province. On one part of the delta
region, "On more than 300,000 mou of the sha-tien (delta fields)
in Pan-yu, at least 40,000 peasants are labouring under a system of multiple sub-renting and extortionate rents in kind —
amounting to from 70 to 80 per cent of the product." (31) For
Kwangtung Province as a whole, however, Chen estimates that

the rent "amounts to 50-57% of the entire harvest." (32)

In 1948-1949, just prior to the change in government, C. K. Yang investigated the village of Nanching, also in the Pearl River Delta, and at that time found that the rent on high-grade land tended to come to 43-50% of the rice yield, that on medium-grade land to 43%, and that on the low-grade unirrigated land (whose productivity was perhaps one-fourth that of the high-grade land) to 25%. (33) Yang also mentions the standard requirement of a rent deposit to be given by the tenant to the landlord as a guarantee against default. The amount, generally retained by the landlord in the case of a long-term tenure, was commonly one-half of a year's rent. (34)

In Ting-hsien, Hopei Province (north China), cash and cash-crop rents were 35-40% of the average gross income from the land, while share rent was regularly 50% of the crop. (35) In some villages of the hsien, a rent deposit equal to one-fifth of the average cash or crop rent was required, imputed interest on which would have amounted to 5-6% of the value of the rent paid. Moreover, the 35-40% figure should be considered in the light of the fact that the rent share tended to be lower in the north, where land productivity was usually lower than in the south.

The most comprehensive compilations of the existing data on the share of agricultural output which land rent constituted are to be found in Materials on China's Modern Agricultural History, Vol. 3, 1927-1937 and in Selected Statistical Materials on China's Modern Economic History, published in Peking (in Chinese) in 1957 and 1955, respectively, as part of the mainland government's efforts to gather systematically the available information on economic conditions in China before the revolution. (36) In the former, the relevant data are given in Table 2-4.

The averages are based on comprehensive province-by-province figures. In the work on modern economic history, comparable data based on different sources are presented. There the systematic provincial figures and national averages are not broken down according to the type of renting system.

Table 2-4

Rent as a Percentage of Output

Land quality	(Fixed) grain rent			Share rent		
	high	middle	low	high	middle	low
Rice farming	46.3	46.2	45.8	51.5	48.0	44.9
Dry farming	45.3	44.6	44.4	47.8	45.3	43.6

Source: Materials on China's Modern Agricultural History, Vol. 3, 1927-1937, pp. 247-248.

Table 2-5

Rent as a Percentage of Output

Land quality	High	Middle	Low
Rice farming	43.6	42.5	44.1
Dry farming	42.6	44.7	46.4

Source: Selected Statistical Materials on China's Modern Economic History, p. 303.

The figures in Tables 2-4 and 2-5 represent simple arithmetic averages of the regions surveyed; it should be kept in mind that there is no way of ascertaining just how representative these regions were.

In Chang-teh County, Honan Province, where cotton was the principal crop and 85% of the land was farmed by tenants, the most prevalent rental arrangement was for the landlord to supply, besides the land, the seed, fertilizer, animals, and tools, in exchange for which he received 80% of the main crop and all the subsidiary crops. (37) Under this arrangement, the landlord also had the right to require labor contributions during the

off-season. Another common arrangement in the same county
was for the landlord to receive 50% of the main crop when he
supplied nothing but land, or 50% of gross output when he supplied one-half the fertilizer input as well. This arrangement
usually involved a three- or four-year contract, but one which
the landlord could, in practice, terminate at any time. It was,
therefore, incumbent upon the tenant to maintain good relations
with the landlord, and although not explicitly required to do so,
he would provide such labor services as repairing the landlord's roof in his free time.

In Tai-an County, Shantung Province, it was most common
to divide all crops equally between the landlord and the tenant. (38) Other arrangements were also observed, whereby the
landlord received only one-half of the main crop or one-half
the main crop and all the subsidiary crops, in the latter of
which cases he typically provided fertilizer or draft animals.

In view of the wide differences in rental systems, practices,
and rates, differences which differentiate even adjacent regions within the same province, and in view of the differences
in concept and the scattered nature of the studies undertaken on
land rent, the available data cannot be averaged or systematically combined to produce an unassailably conclusive figure for
the ratio whose estimation this discussion has been leading up
to, R/Y_{ar} (the share of rent in value added on rented land).
There is ample information, however, on which to base an in-
formed estimate.

The figure which appears most frequently for the rent share
is 50% of "output." Sometimes this included gross output, sometimes only the main crop: there is nothing to indicate which arrangement was more frequent. Where the latter was the case,
the subsidiary crops sometimes went to the landlord, but far
more commonly went to the tenant. When this happened, however, the landlord often received some additional compensation,
which was also the case when the landlord provided some of
the production inputs other than land. Rents higher than 50%
of output generally reflected very high value productivity, a

reflection of high physical productivity or proximity to markets. Prevailing rents appear to have been under 50% about as often as above it; but even where prevailing rents in a locality were 50% or higher, average rents were sometimes lower since inferior land (unirrigated, hilly, infertile, etc.) commonly rented at a considerable discount. The net effect of these various considerations will almost certainly pull the rent share below 50% of gross output. Precisely how much below is hard to say, but a reasonably conservative estimate would put the rent share at 35-45% of gross output, with 40% the most likely figure in this range. Ultimately, this figure is of interest in calculating the share of rent in national income (net domestic product): as the sensitivity tests outlined in the appendix to this chapter show, each 5% difference in the estimate for rent as a share of gross agricultural output results in a difference of about 1.3% in the estimate for the share of rent in national income. Further consideration of some of the studies represented in Table 2-1, however, lends support to the use of the 40% figure.

Buck, among the most reliable of the early investigators, found that an average of 40.5% of gross receipts took the form of rent. While this figure is close to the 40% assumed here, it may have a somewhat downward bias, both because the study excludes south China — where productivity and rentals tended to be somewhat higher — and because there are some indications that rental terms became more severe in the decade following the early 1920s, when the study was made. Buck's 1941 study of Szechwan Province in southwestern China showed 71% of the main crop paid as rent, but only 32% of gross receipts. The unusual difference between these two figures should be considered in light of the numerous special levies which tenants as well as owners paid in Szechwan — a consequence of warlordism and the Nationalist government moving its capital to the province during the war — and the unusual prominence imparted to subsidiary crops by the province's widespread production of opium. Thus the 32% figure is apt to be sharply below the national average.

The study for Chekiang Province also warrants special consideration, since it is a provincewide study undertaken by a prominent economist trained in Western social science methods. The 45% figure is somewhat higher than the figure here, but it should be adjusted downward because, although it is sometimes calculated on the basis of total output, some of the calculations are made on the basis of the principal crop only. While the national data collections (sources 11 and 12) do not specify whether the calculations are made on the basis of total production or principal crop only, the range they indicate, although slightly higher than the 35-45% estimate here, seems consistent with it.

In conclusion, the weight of the evidence presented above suggests, as indicated at the outset of the discussion, that for China as a whole, the tenant, on the average, paid 35-45% of the gross value of his agricultural output (or its cash equivalent) to his landlord as rent, with 40% as the most likely figure in this range. (39)

This figure requires two major adjustments, which must also be estimated, before R/Y_{ar} can be obtained. First, to obtain the value-added figures which the calculation of factor shares requires (in the procedure adopted above), the cost of intermediate inputs (fertilizer, seed, etc.) and depreciation must be subtracted from gross receipts. This will tend to reduce the denominator and increase the ratio. Liu and Yeh estimate such costs as 11% of the gross value of output. (40) This would increase the rental ratio to 44.4% of value added. Second, the supplementary exactions from the tenants, expenses which they had to incur in order to be able to use the land they rented, should also properly be considered part of the rent requirement; and this element, by increasing the numerator, will also tend to increase the ratio.

There is a large assortment of mandatory charges which the tenant had to pay in order to have the privilege of working the land. While not all of them went directly to the landlord, he still benefited by those which did not by being able to pass them on to the tenant. Since they were part of the condition of tenancy, they should properly be considered part of the rent. Although there are many items in this category, the following seven might be especially considered:

1. labor service;
2. gifts to the landlord;
3. intermediary's charges for collection of rent or subletting;
4. special fees and charges;
5. outright dishonesty and/or extortion;
6. the part of the land tax passed on to the tenant;
7. rent deposit. (41)

The first two refer to the gifts or labor service the tenant, depending on the custom of the locality, had to bestow on his landlord on special occasions or at periodic intervals during the year. The third and sixth items represent payments which should properly have been made by the landlord (it is he who chooses to employ the intermediary, and the property tax is a tax on land ownership, not on tenancy) but which were often passed on to the tenant. In effect, the landlord was increasing the rent by such charges in order to meet his own expenses. It is appropriate conceptually, then, to treat them as part of rent. The fourth item includes all sorts of special charges, such as those for transporting the harvested grain from the tenant's farm to the landlord's granary (42); and the fifth is self-explanatory. (43)

The case described above in which the rent deposit was one-half a year's rent indicates the potential burden of rent deposit where the system was in practice. When the deposit is valued in terms of the going interest rates, which averaged 32% a year (44), then the rent deposit itself would add 16% to the value of the rent paid annually. (45) In general, the opportunity costs of making rent deposits were high because interest rates were high. Although precise data on the quantitative importance of each of the items enumerated above is lacking — items which tended to increase the real cost of renting land — some survey information on rent deposits, which is perhaps the most important single item, is available. The Bureau of Statistics of the Legislative Yuan found the deposit system prevalent in 169 hsien of 395 surveyed in twenty-three provinces. (46) This is 43% of the hsien surveyed.

In the absence of more precise information, it is reasonable to suppose that the additional charges which the tenant had to bear must have increased his rent by at least 10%, although this may represent a somewhat conservative estimate, over the 44.4% figure. Adjusting 44.4% upwards by 10% gives a result of 49% of rent as a proportion of value added on rented land. This is R/Y_{ar}, the second of the three ratios which must be determined. The remaining one is Y_{ar}/Y_a, value added on rented land as a proportion of total value added in agriculture.

This figure can be approximated by the proportion of agricultural land subject to tenancy. In making this estimate we must rely primarily on John L. Buck's investigation as representing the most comprehensive scientific survey, based as it is on a study of 16,876 farms spread over twenty-two provinces, although it indicates a considerably lower percentage of tenancy than other contemporary studies. (47) Among the latter, the most significant one, that based on the crop reports of the National Agricultural Research Bureau, is listed below for comparison.

Buck's figures on farm area rented are limited to privately owned land held by individuals, which constituted 93.3% of the total farm area. (48) When considering the proportion of farm land rented, however, there is no reason to exclude the 6.7% of farm land which was not owned by private individuals, including government land (1.0%), school land (0.7%), charity land (0.1%), temple land (1.8%), ancestral land (0.4%), soldier's land (2.3%), and other land (0.4%). (49) This land was basically rented land, the income from which was meant to serve some collective purpose (e.g., the provision of soldiers' pensions or the maintenance of ancestral shrines). During the subsequent land reform, this land was as subject to redistribution as that held by individual landlords. (50) While the total amount of

Table 2-6

The Extent of Tenancy and Farm Area Rented

	Percentage of farmers who are owners, part-owners, and tenants			Percentage of farm area rented (Buck)
	owners	part-owners	tenants	
Buck:				
wheat region	76	18	6	12.7
rice region	38	37	25	40.3
all China	54	29	17	28.7
NARB:				
all China	46	25	29	—

Source: Buck, Land Utilization in China, pp. 194, 196.

land involved was not very large, it was nearly entirely farmed by tenants. If we adjust Buck's data on tenanted land so as to include this portion of the farm land not owned by private individuals, the truly national figure for the proportion of farm land farmed by tenants will rise, accounting for at least some of the discrepancy between Buck's figures and those based on other contemporary surveys. Since private land was 93.3% of total land, and 28.7% of private land was rented out, private land rented out constituted 26.8% of the total land area. Since "public land," or more precisely, land which was not owned by private individuals, rented out constituted 6.7% of the total land area, altogether 33.5% of the total land area was farmed by tenants. (51) The value added on rented land, then, may be regarded as 33.5% of value added in agriculture: $Y_{ar}/Y_a = 33.5\%$.

This ratio completes the information necessary to calculate land rent as a proportion of national income (R/Y). Land rent as a proportion of value added on rented land (R/Y_{ar}) is 49%; value added on rented land as a share of value added in agriculture (Y_{ar}/Y_a) is 33.5%; and value added in agriculture as a

share of total value added in the economy (Y_a/Y) is 65%.
Therefore:

$$\frac{R}{Y} = \frac{R}{Y_{ar}} \times \frac{Y_{ar}}{Y_a} \times \frac{Y_a}{Y}$$

$$= .49 \times .335 \times .65$$

$$= 10.7\%.$$

As a reasonable approximation, then, it may be said that the
principal income flow affected by the land reform in China, that
of land rent, amounted to 10.7% of national income. If the land
formerly worked by tenants had indeed been simply nationalized,
this in itself might have made possible an increase of 10.7 percentage points in the share of national income devoted to investment. (52) Actually, of course, the process did not work
like this. Rather, the land was distributed to poor and landless
peasants, and it became the task of government policy to redirect a portion of the associated incremental income toward
the federal budget through an increase in agricultural taxation
and manipulation of the urban-rural terms of trade.

Farm business profits

It is important to note that the land subject to land reform
was not limited to that owned by landlords but included a portion of the land owned by rich peasants as well. If a man held
more land than he and his family could farm by themselves,
there was no a priori reason why he should rent it out: he
might have chosen instead to hire full-time agricultural laborers to work under his management. Following usual practice,
this arrangement defines the rich peasant as one who, besides
engaging in farming himself, hires one or more full-time agricultural laborers to work the land under his (the owner's) management. Since renting it out would typically require less

effort, he could presumably earn a return at least as great by
managing it himself as by renting it out; he should, in fact,
have been able to earn more by an amount equal to the value
of his management services. This expectation is borne out by
a number of studies, including that of Fei (mentioned above) in
Yunnan:

> Under ordinary circumstances, the nominal (land rent) rate
> of 60% is in reality the maximum and is seldom in effect.
> Even at this high rate, an owner of high-grade land would
> receive a rent of only $4.80 a kung, which is approximately
> $1.00 less than the income he could enjoy by retaining the
> management of his farm and employing others to work it.
> Land rented at the more usual figure of 50% would bring
> $1.50 less. These figures confirm the villagers' observa-
> tion that an owner will find managing his farm much more
> profitable than renting it out. (53)

While land might be rented out if owned by a widow or some-
one in similar circumstances, or because the ownership of
scattered fields made unified management difficult, by far the
most important factor in preferring to rent land was associated
with the opportunity cost of the owner's management services
or his subjective valuation of the cost. As noted above, many
landlords were simultaneously moneylenders, merchants, military officers, or government officials, and others simply set
a high value on their own leisure. (54)

In the absence of such reasons for preferring rental arrangements, owner management was apt to bring a higher return. In
the wheat region, where tenancy was relatively limited, full-
time agricultural laborers constituted a somewhat higher proportion of the agricultural labor force than in the rice region.
For the country as a whole, 15% of the agricultural labor input
was performed by hired labor. (55) The total hired labor input
is not at issue, however, but only that part of it which can be
ascribed to annually hired labor. This is due to the fact that a

large proportion of all farmers, small as well as large, hired labor on a temporary basis to help out during the peak seasons and that land worked in this way was not generally subject to confiscation during the land reform. According to Buck's data, 70.7% of the input of hired farm labor was accounted for by labor hired on a yearly basis (56), so that 0.15 × 0.707, or 10.6% of the total agricultural labor input, was accounted for by labor hired on an annual basis. This seems to be consistent with the estimate that hired agricultural laborers constituted 10.29% of the village population of China (57), keeping in mind that total labor input includes the labor of the farmer's family and that many peasants with insufficient land of their own, either owned or rented, hired themselves out to others on a part-time basis.

With these estimates of hired labor it becomes a relatively simple matter to estimate the income flows associated with the land worked by hired labor, income flows which were subsequently diverted by the land reform. Suppose the surplus produced on the land worked by hired labor, S, is defined as the net value added which is produced on the land minus the total wages paid to those who work it. (58) Then if Y_{ah} is the value added on agricultural land worked by hired labor, and if Y_a and Y are as above, we can write the following equation to find S/Y:

$$\frac{S}{Y} = \frac{S}{Y_{ah}} \times \frac{Y_{ah}}{Y_a} \times \frac{Y_a}{Y}$$

S/Y_{ah} is the net product of the land worked by hired labor minus the total wage payments of those who work it as a proportion of the value added on that land. Y_{ah}/Y_a is the value added on agricultural land cultivated by full-time hired labor as a percentage of value added in agriculture. Y_a/Y, the proportion of value added in the entire economy which can be ascribed to agriculture, has already been found to be 65%. S/Y is the share of national income which is represented by the difference between the net product and total wages of hired agricultural labor.

Previously land rent was found to be 49% of the (agricultural) value added on rented land. Since, according to the argument above, S/Y_{ah} must have been at least this great to have warranted managing one's own land instead of renting it out, we can regard the minimum level of S/Y_{ah}, 49%, as a conservative estimate. (59) Y_{ah}/Y_a can be approximated by the proportion which annually hired labor constituted of the total labor input, which was found above to be 10.6%. (60) Therefore:

$$\frac{S}{Y} = \frac{S}{Y_{ah}} \times \frac{Y_{ah}}{Y_a} \times \frac{Y_a}{Y}$$

$$= .49 \times .106 \times .65$$

$$= 3.4\%.$$

Thus the surplus or net value added by full-time hired labor above and beyond its wages constituted approximately 3.4% of national income.

Interest

A significant share of the return to property in the rural sector took the form of interest. Since all outstanding debts were canceled by the land reform, in evaluating the effects of the land reform it will be helpful to have some idea of the order of magnitude of the income flows involved, and more specifically of the proportion of national income which rural interest payments constituted. Before proceeding with the appropriate calculations, however, I would like to make some general observations on the nature of debt in the rural sector.

First, the problem of debt, which affected owners as well as tenants, although related to that of tenancy is distinct from it. Second, the outstanding debt tended to be somewhat concentrated toward the middle-income levels of the peasantry: the very poorest peasants could rarely provide adequate security for

loans and the richest had no need of them. Third, most loans
were for consumption (to tide a family over until the harvest,
to meet the heavy expenses required for marriages (61) and
funerals, etc.) rather than for productive purposes. According
to Buck, only about one-quarter of farm credit was used for
productive purposes, and most of that took the form of "short-
term" credit to buy fertilizer, implements, animals, and sometimes seed. (62) Buck summarizes his findings on indebtedness
as follows:

> The extent and seriousness of indebtedness varies through-
> out the country. In numerous places the owner tends to lose
> possession of his land to the money lender and at best, to
> become a tenant on his own farm. The tenant sells most of
> his crop immediately after the harvest to pay his debts and
> is almost at once in need of further loans.
>   There is in no sense a national credit market and funds
> available in one part of a province are not to any extent
> available for lending elsewhere, so that interest rates vary
> considerably over short distances. The rate of interest
> paid per month averaged 2.7%, or 32% per year. In the Rice
> Region the rate averaged 2.3% per month or 28% per year,
> while in the Wheat Region it averaged 3.2% per month or
> 38% per year. (63)

Buck found too that 39% of all the farmers he surveyed were
in debt, and that of those in debt the average amount of debt
outstanding was 76 yuan. (64) According to the results of an
extensive survey carried out by the National Agricultural Research Bureau in December 1933, cash-loan indebtedness was
much more widespread, affecting 56% of all farm families; and
the interest burden was slightly heavier for cash loans and
much heavier for grain loans than Buck's data indicate. Table
6 in the Statistical Appendix presents these alternative figures
on a comprehensive province-by-province basis. The fact that
these data were collected later than Buck's, when the effects

of the Great Depression had had more chance to make themselves felt in China, may account for most of the difference. However, the possibility also exists, as I have noted above, that Buck's sample was somewhat biased in such a manner as to include a disproportionate number of richer peasants. (65) Such people would be less likely to fall into debt, and when they did would be able to get loans on more favorable terms, so that the interest rates Buck reports might show a somewhat downward bias. Despite these considerations, in the interests of consistency and because Buck's study employed superior samling techniques, I will use Buck's data as the basis for estimating the national interest payment figures, realizing that the resulting estimates may again be somewhat conservative. In the Appendix to this chapter I test the alternative assumption that 56% of farm families were in debt, as indicated by the NARB data.

If m is the average interest payment per rural household (66), h is the number of rural households, i is the total of rural interest payments, and Y is the national income, then

$$i = mh$$
$$\text{and } \frac{i}{Y} = \frac{mh}{Y}$$

If the average interest rate was 32% per year and the average debt outstanding for families in debt was 76 yuan, then on the average each such family paid 24.32 yuan in interest annually. Since this was true of the 39% of families in debt, $m = .39 \times$ 24.32 yuan, or 9.5 yuan. Assuming that the total population in 1933 was 500 million (67), that 90% of the population lived in rural areas (68), and that the mean family size for the rural population was the same as the 5.2 persons Buck found for farm families (69), $h = .9 \times 500$ million $\div$ 5.2, or 86,538,000 households. Y in 1933, as shown by Table 2 in the Statistical Appendix, was 28.86 billion yuan. Therefore:

$$i = mh$$
$$= 9.5 \text{ yuan} \times 86{,}538{,}000$$
$$= 822 \text{ million yuan}$$

$$\text{and } \frac{i}{Y} = \frac{mh}{Y}$$

$$= \frac{822 \text{ million yuan}}{28{,}860 \text{ million yuan}}$$

$$= 2.8\%.$$

Thus the flow of rural interest payments constituted 2.8% of national income in 1933.

Taxes and special levies

To see the process of institutional change in agriculture clearly, some idea of the initial levels of rural taxation will be helpful. Land taxes, of course, are also of interest because they claimed a portion of the return to land, a portion fairly readily identifiable. Even more important though is the fact that land taxes were at the center of an entire network of rural social relations and institutional practices which go far toward explaining the limitations on capital formation during the period prior to 1949.

Prior to 1940 farm land taxes were not paid to the central government but were divided between the hsien (county) and provincial governments. According to Buck's data, "On medium grade land, the average tax paid by farmers in 47 localities was [Chin.] $6.34 per acre. In the Wheat Region the total tax on medium land was $5.16 per acre compared to $8.24 in the Rice Region." (70) Taking these figures, which represent the 1929-1933 average, as representative of the nation as a whole and multiplying the average figure by the 217 million acres of farm land (71) suggests that hsien and provincial governments would have received land taxes of Chinese $1,376 million yuan

yearly, or 4.8% of China's net domestic product in 1933 (72) —
if all tax obligations had been paid and if all had found their
proper destination. In actuality, receipts and expenditures by
all levels of government, including the national government,
did not encompass such a large proportion of national income. (73) Furthermore, land taxes did not enter into the
budget of the national government and constituted a minority
of provincial government receipts, so that the difference between the land taxes that should have been paid and the land
taxes received was quite considerable.

A large part of the discrepancy can be accounted for by the
successful evasion of taxation by those landowners who kept
perhaps one-third of China's arable land unregistered and thus
off the tax rolls. (74) The existence of the commissioned tax
collecting agents or tax farmers, described by Chen Han-seng
as follows, further clarifies the discrepancy:

> The actual sums collected by these agents are several
> times, sometimes as much as ten times, what the Government receives. This almost unbelievable statement has
> been verified in a number of instances. Of course, it must
> be realized that it does not imply a fantastically successful
> peculation and enrichment of a few individuals: as taxes and
> tolls multiply, a whole army of collectors spring into being
> to prey upon the people, none of them big men as rascals
> go in China, but, although each overcharges by 500 or even
> 900 per cent, more like a swarm of locusts than a herd of
> bisons. (75)

The land-tax figures do not include the miscellaneous sales,
transit, animal slaughter, and other local taxes of every variety and description which proliferated during this period.

The amounts involved were thus quite substantial and would
be swelled still further if we considered them together with the
proceeds of banditry, a proposition that is less strange than
may appear at first sight. In some regions of Kwangtung, for

example, bandits issued "black tickets" to prevent cultivating
or harvesting by peasants who failed to pay them the required
fees. (76) Tawney observes that

> over a large area of China, the rural population suffers
> horribly through the insecurity of life and property. It is
> taxed by one ruffian who calls himself a general, by another,
> by a third, and, when it has bought them off, still owes taxes
> to the Government; in some places actually more than
> twenty years' taxation has been paid in advance. It is
> squeezed by dishonest officials. It must cut its crops at the
> point of the bayonet, and hand them over without payment to
> the local garrison, though it will starve without them. It is
> forced to grow opium in defiance of the law, because its
> military tyrants can squeeze heavier taxation from opium
> than from rice or wheat, and make money, in addition, out
> of the dens where it is smoked. It pays blackmail to the
> professional bandits in its neighborhood; or it resists, and,
> a year later, when the bandits have assumed uniform, sees
> its villages burned to the ground. (77)

Thirty-four percent of the villages responding to Buck's inquiry
regarding factors affecting living standards noted banditry, a
greater percentage than those mentioning drought and flood. (78)
Buck himself, who is usually quite conservative in such matters,
observes that

> in the Szechwan Rice Area, however, taxes of five dollars
> or more per acre must be considered definitely high. In
> recent years the local warlords in Szechwan have exploited
> the farmers mercilessly, in some cases collecting taxes for
> many years in advance. In some instances, excessively high
> taxes have been levied for the purpose of forcing the farm-
> ers to grow opium which is the only crop which will yield
> enough cash income per acre to pay the excessive taxes.
> This situation has also existed in parts of the Winter Wheat-

Millet Area and helps to explain the unusually high taxation prevailing there.

More unfortunate than the high level of taxes prevailing in the Winter Wheat-Millet, the Szechwan Rice, and parts of other areas is the fact that a large proportion of the tax collected by the Hsien Governments from the farmers is not used for purposes which are of any value to the farmers, but goes for the support of the local politicians and private armies. (79)

Another source with no vested interest in exaggerating the harshness of rural conditions, the office of the Pacification Commission in Kwangtung, whose task it was to stamp out the communist movement, issued the following proclamation in April 1933:

The work of reconstruction in this province has been steadily progressing during the last few years; the burden on the people is also getting increasingly heavy. Numerous tax bureaus have been established in every locality, extracting money under all sorts of cleverly named surtaxes, and making requisitions for various pretended military purposes. These miscellaneous levies far exceed the tax proper; they satisfy the rapacity of the local gentry, but hardly at all con-tribute toward the cost of public works. This condition must be alleviated, if the people's ability to pay taxes is to be preserved. (80)

These various observations serve to indicate both the actual social conditions prevailing in rural China and the consensus of observers with different viewpoints concerning them. The picture that emerges is one of a small army of individuals with variegated yet overlapping roles, dependent for their live-lihood on extracting the maximum possible share of the output of farmers and other productive workers. The gentry were landlords and merchants; the bandits became soldiers and vice

versa; the landlords were usurers; the merchants were commissioned by the government to collect taxes, and the taxes
collected made it possible to support local warlords and to create official jobs for the gentry. This is of course a picture
drawn with broad strokes: there were essential functions performed by each of these groups (even banditry helped ease the
rural unemployment problem); but these functions were perhaps
dwarfed by the magnitude of resources extracted for which no
useful social or economic functions were performed.

It is worthwhile keeping in mind that most of the practices
under discussion were part of a self-contained system which
the central government was unable to affect or could influence
only marginally, even when it had the will to do so. It is clear
that at least some of the public officials were conscious of the
seriousness of the conditions they confronted, but such officials remained powerless to do anything about them.

The problem and potential this situation created for economic development can be grasped readily in terms of the
class model I have presented in Chapter One.* It will be useful
to recall that the four groups distinguished there were (1) owners of property (land and capital); (2) producers of luxury goods
and services; (3) producers of subsistence goods and services;
and (4) producers of capital goods, with the surplus produced
by class 3 above its own consumption serving to maintain the
other three classes. Class 2 is dependent upon and essentially
a derivative of class 1: a reduction in the size of class 1 means,
ceteris paribus, a commensurate reduction in the size of
class 2. This aspect of the model was quite closely approximated by conditions in China, as the discussion of this chapter
should have made clear. The services included in class 2 are
not only those for consumption purposes but those which served
to maintain the traditional social structure — and thus the position of those in class 1 — as well.

The nonproductive rural groups to which I have been referring

---

*See p. 21.

must be classified in class 1 or 2. A reduction in the consumption of these classes (81) could be accompanied by an expansion of employment in class 4 if the "leakage" of increased consumption in class 3 can be restrained. To uncover the hidden saving potential in the rural economy, then, it would be useful to have a comprehensive picture of the income flows entering class 1 (and the typically derivative ones entering class 2).

For those areas within the agricultural sector for which the available data make systematic treatment feasible, I have tried to estimate the relevant income flows as a share of national income. Recognizing that the estimates could not be exact, but at the same time taking into account the fact that the identification of the correct orders of magnitude would be sufficient to throw considerable light on the role of institutional change in altering the existing income flows and in bringing about an increase in the national savings ratio, I have found that land rent constituted 10.7% of national income; the surplus produced by annually hired labor above its own consumption 3.4%; and rural interest payments 2.8%. The sum of these categories is 16.9% of national income.

Land taxes constituted another category of payments which were supported by the net product of agriculture. If all such tax obligations had been paid and if all had found their proper destination in public coffers, the sums involved would have amounted to 4.8% of China's net domestic product. Since about one-third of the arable land was not on the tax rolls, the payments made came to only 3.2% of net domestic product, of which 1.1% can be ascribed to landlords and 2.1% to owner-farmers (in accordance with their respective landholding shares). Of these payments, only a small fraction wound up in the hands of public authorities, the rest going to tax farmers, warlords, and so forth. While only the landlord share of these payments (about 1.1% of NDP) constitutes part of the property share proper (and this is included in the 10.7% which land rent constituted of NDP), in the Chinese context the entire amount represented intrinsic elements in the preservation and perpetuation of the property-owning system. By bringing all land onto the tax rolls and by eliminating leakages into private hands, the land reform released sources of development financing which went beyond the diversion of property-income flows proper. (82)

While the post-1949 changes in those income flows for which estimates have been made will be dealt with in some detail in Chapter Three, one summary observation of a general nature can be made at this point. It is that the size of the income flows entering classes 1 and 2 constituted a substantial portion of national income and therefore represented a considerable, if hidden, potential in the rural economy of China both for increasing the rate of capital formation (financing increased employment and output in class 4) and for increasing peasant consumption (raising the real income of the producers of subsistence goods in class 3). This belies the conventional view that China was simply too poor to finance her own development without intolerably squeezing her peasantry.

Rural investment

Since it is the changes in the level of investment in the economy that are at issue, it will be necessary to have some idea of the levels of investment prevailing in the rural economy prior to 1949. To the extent that the recipients of the property-share components of national income used their income for investment purposes, any institutional reforms which redirected these income flows toward public authorities or other groups in the economy would, in the first instance, have the effect of reducing investment to the same extent. As can be inferred readily from the aggregate national investment data cited in the Statistical Appendix, however, this effect cannot have been significant, with net domestic investment constituting 1.72% of net domestic expenditure in 1933.

While the exact level of agricultural investment in the 1930s remains an open question, it is clear that the amount was not substantial. There was no distinct trend in agricultural output during this period, and farming techniques remained essentially unchanged, suggesting that whatever investment may have taken place was quite limited. Liu and Yeh have assumed that gross investment and depreciation both ran at a 2% level, leaving the level of net investment in agriculture at zero. (83) This estimate appears the most reasonable and consistent with the limited information available and consequently will be adopted here. While there may in actuality have been some net disinvestment or a small amount of (positive) net investment, the potential error involved in assuming a zero level of net investment cannot be very large.

The question of the exact extent to which saving in the agricultural sector financed investment in the industrial sector also remains open; but once again, any such flow of funds cannot have been significant: most industrial investment was financed from retained earnings, supplemented by funds from foreigners, merchants, and political-military figures. While some landlords were merchants and industrialists, this situation was almost invariably brought about when the latter groups bought land, rather than the other way around. Once again, these considerations must be viewed in the light of the 1.72% of net domestic product which investment constituted in 1933. To assume that industrial investment was not financed by savings in the agricultural sector is most reasonable; but even if this estimate should be wide of the mark — and the data available are simply not sufficient to confirm it or deny it definitively — the discrepancy cannot be of material significance and is unlikely to exceed 0.5% of net domestic product in any event.

Summary

Thus the land reform redirected income flows amounting to

16.9% of net domestic product (NDP) which had formerly gone
to the owners of property in the agricultural sector, of which
1.1% of NDP had nominally taken the form of (agricultural) tax
payments. In addition, owner-farmers made nominal tax payments equal to 2.1% of NDP. In the absence of government investment activity in the 1930s, these "tax" payments made no
significant contribution to net investment activity at that time.
By redirecting these income flows, the land reform made potentially available for investment finance about 19% of net
domestic product — at zero opportunity cost from the standpoint of investment foregone. Just how much of this potentiality was realized, in accordance with the schema outlined in
Chapter One, is the subject of the next chapter. Before proceeding to that, however, relating the results obtained here to
the equations presented in Chapter One should further clarify
the ensuing discussion.

Equation (3) on page 16 of Chapter One, reproduced below,
shows the three principal components of property-owner income (Y_t): rental income (rQ), farm business profits $(r'Q)$,
and interest income (iL_{tp}). The data developed in this chapter
make it possible to estimate these magnitudes in 1933 prices.

$$Y_t = rQ + r'Q + iL_{tp} = C_t + S_t + M_t \tag{3}$$

Since $Y_a = .89Q$ (84) and $Y_a = 18.76$ billion yuan (85), $Q = 21.08$
billion yuan. This is the gross value of agricultural output.
While the rent share of net output (value added) on rented land
was estimated in this chapter as 0.49, as a share of the gross
output on rented land, where supplementary exactions properly
considered a part of the rent are included, it is 0.44. (86) If
we assume that the share of the gross output produced on
rented land in total agricultural output is the same as the share
of agricultural value added produced on rented land, or 0.335,
then the proportion of gross agricultural output paid as land
rent is 0.44 × 0.335, or 0.147: this is r in the equation above.
r' is the share of gross agricultural output produced on land

worked by hired labor above and beyond the cost of such labor. According to the argument developed more fully in the text, the return from working land with hired labor under one's own management must have been at least as great as that available from renting it, or the landowner would have preferred to rent his land. A conservative estimate for r', then, will be 0.44 × .106, or .0466, if we assume that the share of gross agricultural output produced on land worked by hired labor was the same as the share of (full-time) hired labor in the agricultural labor force (10.6%).

i was found in the discussion above to average 32%, and the level of loans outstanding (L_{t_p}) is 76 yuan (the average loan for those families in debt) × 0.39 (the proportion of rural households in debt) × 86,538,000 (the number of rural households). Accordingly:

Y_t = 0.147(21.08 billion yuan) + 0.0466(21.08 billion yuan)
+ 0.32(76 yuan × 0.39 × 86.538 million)

Y_t = 3,099 million yuan + 982 million yuan + 821 million yuan

Y_t = 4,902 million yuan.

The principal impact of the land reform was in redirecting this income flow of some 4.9 billion yuan (out of 1933's net domestic product of 28.86 billion yuan [87]) away from the owners of property and, initially, into the hands of the poorer peasants.

While M_t, consisting of land taxes paid by landlords, has been estimated at 1.1% of NDP, or 317 million yuan, it is not feasible to estimate with any great degree of precision the component parts of the uses to which property owners put their disposable income (C_t and S_t). It is possible, however, to state with confidence that the portion of their saving which found its way into productive investment was inconsequential, and therefore that the opportunity cost of diverting their income was, from the standpoint of net national saving, negligible. The greater part of a small S_t was counterbalanced by the dissaving of peasants. Any part of the windfall gain the poorer peasants received as a result of the land reform which public policy could reextract and use to finance investment, therefore, could stand as a net addition to national saving. The success of the efforts to secure a portion of this windfall to finance investment is the subject of the next chapter.

Notes

1) As noted in Chapter One, such people were called "running dogs" by Mao Tse-tung. We have no way of knowing just how large this group was, but it was sufficiently important to warrant a special term and received frequent mention in social commentaries of the period.

2) In a study Fei Hsiao-tung undertook in a village south of Lake Tai in the Yangtze Valley, for example, he found that the agents employed by the landlords' collective rent-collecting bureau were entrusted with police power by the district government. Peasant Life in China (London, 1939), p. 188.

3) See the discussion of agricultural investment in the "Rural Investment" section of this chapter (pages 77-78).

4) The argument here is not meant to oversimplify the complex interaction between economic organization and innovation. When productivity-increasing innovations take place, rentier landlords may become entrepreneurial farmers or give way to them, as may be happening in parts of the Philippines with the introduction of IR-8 rice. Thus the argument is not of innate deficiencies in China's landlords but simply that their behavior, given existing conditions, was not conducive to growth.

5) Earthbound China (Chicago, 1945), pp. 245-48.

6) Ibid., pp. 246-47.

7) Education beyond primary school commonly involved attending a boarding school and thus was beyond the reach of ordinary villagers. While it is possible to treat expenditure

on education as a form of investment under certain circumstances, I do not do so here. The most important reason is
that I am concerned with directly productive material investments, investments such as are ordinarily incorporated in
national income accounts; education is not included in the investment rates whose changes I am seeking to explain. Other
considerations include the fact that much of the educational
expense represented luxury consumption — as for student uni-
forms — and much of the expenditure was directed toward
securing the status of the student and his family rather than
the economic development of the nation. I would, moreover,
be extremely loathe under any circumstances to treat expenditures at military academies, a large component of educational
expenditure, as a form of investment.

8) Earthbound China, pp. 85, 91-94.

9) Asian Rural Society, p. 91.

10) Buck, Land Utilization in China, p. 350.

11) Tawney, Land and Labour in China (London, 1932), p. 54.
Tawney's figure is based on local studies available at the time
he was writing, in 1930-1931.

12) In a 1941 study carried out by Buck in Szechwan Province,
the average farm price per shih tan of polished rice was 74.07
yuan; the wholesale marketing price was 190.91 yuan. Buck
estimates the normal transport and marketing cost at 13.76
yuan, the business costs and normal profit of merchants at
28.10 yuan. The difference between these normal costs and
the wholesale price, representing speculator profits, was 74.98
yuan, or more than the farmer himself received. This of course
reflects wartime conditions, but war and crisis were never far
from Chinese agriculture in the period under review. Buck,
Agricultural Survey of Szechuan Province, China (Chungking,
1943).

13) The Economy of the Chinese Mainland, p. 66. Also see
Statistical Appendix, Table 2.

14) Buck, Land Utilization in China, p. 198.

15) Buck, Chinese Farm Economy, p. 149. It should be noted

that these are total receipts before any deductions for operating expenses.

16) Buck, Agricultural Survey of Szechuan Province, China, p. 2.

17) Ibid., p. 5. The singularly small share which the main crop (rice) comprised of gross agricultural output in Szechwan reflects largely the extensive growing of opium in that province.

18) Agricultural Survey of Szechuan Province, China, p. 6.

19) China, Ministry of Industries, Bureau of Foreign Trade, Hunan, An Economic Survey, p. 8.

20) The following, for example, describes the situation in Foping in northwest Hopei, bordering Shansi: "The collection of grain rent here as elsewhere is not exempt from the abuses of the landlord who, when taking rent, always uses a measure 10 or 20% larger than the standard one. Any dispute regarding measurement inevitably results in the eviction of the tenant." Agrarian China: Selected Source Materials from Chinese Authors (London, 1939), p. 19. (This work is a collection of essays by different authors which appeared in Chinese journals in Chinese in the 1930s and which have been compiled and translated by the research staff of the Secretariat, Institute of Pacific Relations.)

Dishonesty, of course, was not the exclusive prerogative of any one class. Tenants under the share-rent system often attempted to conceal grain; those under the cash or cash-crop system to underestimate harvests in hopes of securing a reduction in their rent (Buck, Chinese Farm Economy, p. 150). The point remains, however, that with local government left in the hands of the gentry — comprised essentially of the landowning class — and with China's high man-land ratio, the relative capacity of the two parties to excel in duplicity was distinctly unequal.

21) Agrarian China, p. 17.

22) Ibid., p. 31.

23) Ibid., p. 44.

24) Ibid., pp. 78-79.

25) China Year Book 1934, p. 767. It is true that a degree of reciprocity in obligations existed. While in some places it was customary for the tenant to entertain the landlord at a feast at harvest time, sometimes it was expected of the landlord. Here too, however, the reciprocity cannot have been great in relation to the onus on the tenant. It was common, for example, for landlords to employ agents to collect their rents, and the tenants had to "treat them well" to be sure of maintaining their tenancy. And landlords did not customarily leave deposits with tenants or pay fees of any sort to them.

26) Tawney's Land and Labour in China, published in 1932, provides a helpful summary of some of the most important investigations of land-tenure conditions undertaken prior to that date.

27) Fei Hsiao-tung and Chang Chih-I, Earthbound China: A Study of Rural Economy in Yunnan (Chicago, 1945), p. 75.

28) Ibid., pp. 154, 157.

29) Ibid., p. 224.

30) Chen Han-seng, Landlord and Peasant in China (New York, 1936), pp. 60-62.

31) Ibid., p. 22. This example is but one of many which indicate the close relationship between the level of rents and both land productivity and proximity to markets.

32) Ibid., p. ix.

33) C. K. Yang, A Chinese Village in Early Communist Transition, p. 49. Reprinted in Chinese Communist Society: The Family and the Village (Cambridge, Mass., 1965).

34) Ibid., pp. 50-51.

35) Sidney D. Gamble, Ting Hsien: A North China Rural Community (Stanford, 1968), p. 215. The data for this county should be regarded with the fact in mind that it was a center of nationally supported improvement efforts.

36) The Chinese titles and chief editors of the works are respectively: Chung-kuo chin-tai nung-yeh shih tzu-liao, ti-san-chi, 1927-1937, ed. Chang Yu-i, and Chung-kuo chin-tai ching-chi shih t'ung-chi tzu-liao hsüan-chi, ed. Yen Chung-

p'ing. Hereafter the works will be referred to by the translated (English) titles cited in the text.

37) This and the following data concerning Chang-teh County are from the South Manchurian Railway Co., Research Division, Report on the Agricultural Situation in North China: Chang-teh Hsien, Honan (Tokyo, 1940), pp. 69-73 (in Japanese).

38) This and the following data concerning Tai-an County are from the South Manchurian Railway Co., North China Economic Research Institute, Report on the Agricultural Situation in North China, Vol. II: Tai-an Hsien, Shantung (Dairen, 1940), p. 30 (in Japanese).

39) This estimate is lower than that cited by Albert Feuerwerker, who writes, "The failure of the Kuomintang policy of limiting rents to 37.5% of the main crops is well known, and most observers agree that rent absorbed at least 50% of the tenants' annual farm produce." The Chinese Economy, 1912-1949 (Ann Arbor, 1968), p. 36. Feuerwerker does not make clear, however, whether he is referring to gross or net output and whether subsidiary crops are included in his figure.

40) See equation (1), page 16, and related discussion.

41) While almost all descriptions of tenancy conditions in China in the 1930s touch upon one or more of these items, the following references are cited for illustrative purposes. (1) Chen, Landlord and Peasant in China; Agrarian China, pp. 18-19; Materials on China's Modern Agricultural History, Vol. 3, 1927-1937, p. 249; Selected Statistical Materials on China's Modern Economic History, pp. 295-99; Tawney, Land and Labour in China, p. 65. (2) China Year Book 1934, p. 767; Landlord and Peasant in China. (3) and (4) Agrarian China; Landlord and Peasant in China. (5) Agrarian China. (7) Selected Statistical Materials, p. 308; Agrarian China, pp. 96-101; Yang, A Chinese Village in Early Communist Transition, pp. 50-51; Landlord and Peasant in China.

42) Essential auxiliary services had to be maintained after the revolution too, of course, but it appears that landowner charges were often above the opportunity costs of the factors

employed. Note too that some of the services were required
only for the given production relations: the cost of rent collection especially disappeared with landlordism.

43) Dishonesty was not, of course, a landowner monopoly,
but that of the tenant was typically constrained by the fact that
the risks he ran were much greater. See Note 20 above.

44) See the discussion of interest rate levels on pages
68-71 of this chapter.

45) Except for the early 1930s, inflation marked most of the
period between 1911 and 1949. To the extent that inflation took
place, the real value of rent deposits made in prior years decreased. On the other hand, when and if deposits were returned,
their real value decreased with inflation, adding capital loss to
the tenants' burden in making such deposits.

46) Feuerwerker, p. 36.

47) Since much of Buck's actual survey work was undertaken by investigators who, like any of the educated in traditional China, tended to come from the wealthier segments of
the population, it is possible that a rich peasant bias has crept
into his results. If so, this might be reflected in underestimates
of tenancy and interest rates, and in overestimates of the full-
time hired labor input and tax payments. Buck himself hints at
such a possibility when he writes, "Instructions to investigators
were to select farms and families on the basis of taking all the
farms or families in a village, or, in the case of a large village,
by taking them consecutively along typical streets or sections
of the village. In many localities, this did not prove feasible,
and for this reason there may be some bias in the data, probably resulting in the selection of samples better than average."
(Land Utilization in China, p. ix.) Feuerwerker argues that
"Buck's data underestimate the incidence of tenancy largely
because they give inadequate weight to the South, where tenancy was much more widespread than in North and Central
China." (Feuerwerker, p. 35.) It is also possible that the impact of the Great Depression in China is more fully indicated
by the 1934 National Agricultural Research Bureau (NARB)

tenancy figures, which appear in the text in Table 2-6; although Buck's data were gathered from 1929 to 1933, many of the observations were made in 1930-1931.

48) Buck, Land Utilization in China, p. 193.

49) Ibid., p. 193. In view of Professor Buck's principal interest in the problems of farm management and living standards and patterns, it would seem strange from the standpoint of his own objectives that he saw fit to segregate privately owned land from other land when considering the extent of tenancy in China.

50) See Section 2, Article 3, of the Agrarian Reform Law of the People's Republic of China, promulgated June 30, 1950. Included in S. B. Thomas, Recent Political and Economic Developments in China (New York, 1950), p. 91. For concrete instances, see the works of Yang and Hinton cited in Chapter Three.

51) As indicated on page 3, 44% of the arable land area was redistributed. This is in excess of the share, indicated here, of the land farmed by tenants. The difference is accounted for by the "excess" land expropriated from rich peasants (land in excess of what they could farm themselves with a modest amount of assistance), land seized from those who collaborated with the Japanese military occupation, and the fact that in some instances any land in excess of the local average holding was subject to seizure. For a fuller discussion, see the description of the redistribution process in Chapter Three.

52) Assuming no impact on work incentives and neglecting, for the moment, the share of the land tax payments borne by landlords. The land tax will be dealt with separately below, but it might be noted here that the portion of the land tax which found its way into investment was negligible. The statement in the text further assumes that ex-landlords would have to engage in productive activity to secure the means for their necessary consumption, so that no portion of the increase in state revenues would have to be set aside for this purpose.

53) Fei, Earthbound China, p. 75.

54) Chen Han-seng, in The Present Agrarian Problem in China (Shanghai, 1933), p. 19, describes the results of an investigation of the chief profession of big landlords in Kiangsu as follows: "Each of the 514 big landlords investigated owns from 1,000 to 60,000 Mow; and 374 of them have their chief profession definitely known. Most of the remaining 140 are not ascertained as to their profession, but only a very few of them are purely rent collectors. Of the total of 374, 44.39% are military and civil officers of different ranks, 34.49% are pawn shop and money shop owners and individual usurers, 17.91% are shop keepers and traders, only 3.21% are shareholders of factories. Elsewhere in China the landlords rarely become factory shareholders; they practice usury most naturally. A comparatively higher percentage of landlord-officials, however, may be found in the Northwestern and Northeastern provinces, and that of landlord-merchants in Hopei, Shantung, Hupeh and other provinces where trade has been better developed."

55) Buck, Land Utilization in China, p. 293. While the possible rich-peasant bias in Buck's estimates may have inflated this figure somewhat, this estimate is more conservative than that provided by Buck in Chinese Farm Economy, p. 234, where he found that hired labor represented 19.5% of the total farm labor cost, including the imputed cost of the operator's labor.

56) Buck, Chinese Farm Economy, p. 235.

57) Selected Statistical Materials on China's Modern Economic History, p. 263.

58) S includes the return to all factors of production other than hired labor: land, capital, and the management services of the owner.

59) While the actual level must be higher than this, a part of it represents the return to the management services of the owner. As my focus is on the relevant property share, I have deliberately chosen the minimum level in estimating S/Y_{ah}. In the Appendix to this chapter, however, the effect of a higher estimate on S/Y is worked out.

60) This assumes that the production function and factor

inputs are the same, on the average, for land worked with hired labor as for agriculture as a whole, an assumption which appears basically justified in the light of Chinese conditions; hired farm hands carried out much the same types of activity as others engaged in farming, and large-scale mechanized and plantation-type farming were insignificant. It should be noted, however, that the average productivity per worker was much greater on large farms than on small ones (Buck, Land Utilization in China, p. 283). To the extent that hired labor was more likely to be found on the larger farms, its productivity is apt to have been higher than average, creating a conservative bias in the estimates in the text.

61) A wedding cost four months' family income and exceeded the yearly income of hired farm laborers (Land Utilization in China, p. 19), many of whom could not, accordingly, afford to marry.

62) Ibid., p. 461.

63) Ibid., p. 463.

64) Ibid., p. 464.

65) See the discussion in Note 47.

66) Assuming, as an admitted approximation, that the average for all rural households is the same as that for farm households. In the Appendix to this chapter, the consequences of an alternative assumption, that rural debt was restricted to farm families, are explored.

67) Liu and Yeh, p. 171. The authors' argument that previous population estimates were too low is convincing.

68) Official government estimates for 1949 to 1957 inclusive, cited in Liu and Yeh, p. 212, show a gradual decrease in the rural percent of the population from 89.6% to 85.8% with the advance of industrialization and urbanization. The assumption that 90% of the population lived in rural areas in 1933 is based on the 1949 figure.

69) Land Utilization in China, p. 368.

70) Ibid., p. 325. These figures are expressed in Chinese dollars or yuan.

71) Ibid., p. 165.

72) See Table 2 in the Statistical Appendix.

73) See the data on national and local government budgets in the Statistical Appendix.

74) Letter from John L. Buck to Arthur Young, cited in the latter's China's Wartime Finance and Inflation, p. 22.

75) Landlord and Peasant in China, p. 74.

76) Ibid., p. 81.

77) Land and Labour in China, p. 73.

78) Land Utilization in China, p. 472.

79) Ibid., p. 328.

80) Cited in Chen, Landlord and Peasant in China, p. 73.

81) That the income going to these classes (see p. 21 for definitions) is reduced does not mean, of course, that the people who constituted them must starve. It does mean that all in class 1 and many in class 2 must join one of the other two classes for a livelihood. A carpenter engaged in building a luxurious residence for a landowner before the revolution, for example, might be engaged in factory construction afterwards: he still carries on the same trade, but the change in the object of his activities means he has left class 2 and joined class 4.

82) The land-tax payments constitute only a portion, though a significant one, of the vast shadow-world of semilegal practices which existed in the countryside prior to the land reform and which are not amenable to systematic aggregation.

83) Liu and Yeh, p. 73n. The assumption of a zero level of net investment implies that some (positive) gross investment was taking place. Liu, in an earlier work, China's National Income 1931-36: An Exploratory Study (Washington, D.C., 1946), cites Buck's estimate in Chinese Farm Economy that gross agricultural capital formation was 2% of gross agricultural production. I see no reason to dispute this figure. Ou Pao-san estimates an even lower, actually negative, level of net investment in the entire economy in 1933: minus 397 million yuan. "A New Estimate of China's National Income," Journal of Political Economy LIV (December 1946), 550-51. Ou's work,

however, is less comprehensive and considerably less reliable than that of Liu and Yeh.

84) See equation (1), Chapter One, p. 16.

85) See Statistical Appendix, Table 2.

86) Forty percent of gross output plus an additional 10% of this figure to reflect supplementary exactions. See the discussion in the text.

87) See Table 2 in the Statistical Appendix. The property share here works out to almost 17% of net domestic product, due to rounding both here and in the earlier estimates.

Appendix:
Effects of alternative assumptions on the final estimate

1.	Rent as % of gross output value	R/Y_{ar} (%)	R/Y (%)		$(R/Y)'$ (%)
a)	35	43	9.4	a')	7.9
b)	40	49	10.7	b')	9.0
c)	45	55	12.0	c')	10.1
d)	50	61	13.3	d')	11.2

Note:

$(R/Y)'$ presents the 1933 rent share valued in 1952 prices, according to which agriculture constituted 55% of net domestic product (see Statistical Appendix, Table 2), rather than the 65% it constituted in current prices.

2.	S/Y_{ah} (%)	S/Y (%)		$(S/Y)'*$ (%)
a)	49†	3.4	a')	2.9
b)	55	3.8	b')	3.2

Notes:

*As in the case of $(R/Y)'$ above, $(S/Y)'$ is calculated in terms of 1952 prices.

†As indicated in Chapter Two of the text, the 49% estimate for S/Y_{ah} was conservatively based on the assumption that the surplus obtainable from managing one's own land was at least as great as that obtainable from renting it out. Any return to the managerial contribution of owners would increase the percentage. Cases 2b and 2b' show how the results might vary with a modest managerial return incorporated in S/Y_{ah}.

3.

	% of China's households to whom rural indebtedness ratios apply	% of rural households in debt	Average interest payment per rural household	$i/Y(\%)$
a)	77	39	9.5 yuan	2.4
b)	77	56	13.6 yuan	3.5
c)	90	39	9.5 yuan	2.8
d)	90	56	13.6 yuan	4.1

Notes:

In the text I have assumed that rural indebtedness affected all rural families (90% of the total population). If only the agricultural families were in debt (the available surveys cover only these families), then only 77% of the total population would have been affected.

The National Agricultural Research Bureau studies of agricultural indebtedness showed 56% of farm families in debt (see text) as opposed to Buck's 39% estimate, which I have used. Cases 3b and 3d show how the higher estimate would affect the results.

4. Combined estimates, summary table:

		R/Y	S/Y	i/Y	I*	II[†]
a)	low (1a'+2a'+3a)	7.9	2.9	2.4	13.2	15.3
b)	medium [‡] (1b+2a+3c)	10.7	3.4	2.8	16.9	19.0
c)	high (1d+2b+3d)	13.3	3.8	4.1	21.2	23.3

Notes:

*I is the property share of national income affected by the land reform.

[†]II = I + agricultural tax payments not included in I (those made by owner-farmers). These were 2.1% of net domestic product.

[‡]The medium estimate reflects the component estimates found most reasonable in the discussion of the text.

5. Sensitivity tests:

Estimate in question	% change	Effect on final estimate of the property share*
a) Rent as % of gross output value	5	1.3%
b) Share of agriculture in net domestic product	5	1.1%
c) S/Y_{ah}	5	0.3%
d) % of rural households in debt	5	0.4%

*Estimated at 16.9% of net domestic product in the text and in the medium estimate above. The figures in this column show the change in the property share as a % of NDP when the component estimates change as indicated.

CHAPTER THREE

The contribution of the
land reform to investment finance

By August 1952 land reform had, in the main, been completed throughout China. Before the founding of the People's Republic of China on October 1, 1949, land reform had been carried out widely in the liberated districts, and in the next three years it covered areas with a rural population of some 300 million persons. Including the redistribution which took place before October 1, 1949, about 300 million peasants with little or no land (60 to 70% of the nation's agricultural population) received 47.2 million hectares of arable land, most of which had belonged to landlords. (1) This represents 44% of the 107.9 million hectares under cultivation in 1952. (2) The minister of agriculture estimated in 1952 that from the 700 million mou of land redistributed (3) the landlords had collected annually more than 30 million tons of grain as rent from the peasants. (4) My intention here is to assess the impact of this massive land redistribution on the national savings-investment ratio. It may clarify the matter, however, to consider first the ways in which the agricultural sector might have contributed to the financing of investment and to consider the impact of land reform per se within this context.

In general, the contribution of agriculture to national investment may assume a number of different forms. First, it may appear as self-financed investment within the agricultural sector. Second, it may involve increased tax payments, which enlarge the government budget and make possible an increase in public investment. Third, it may have the same consequences by increasing the profits of government purchasing agencies. Fourth, in contributing (via its purchases) to the profits of firms in the industrial sector, agriculture can contribute to direct investment, or, if the profits pass through the government budget via taxes or profit remittances of publicly owned firms, it can contribute indirectly to public investment. Fifth, saving may take the form of the accumulation of financial assets. These relationships are summarized in the following flow chart of agriculture's potential contribution to saving:

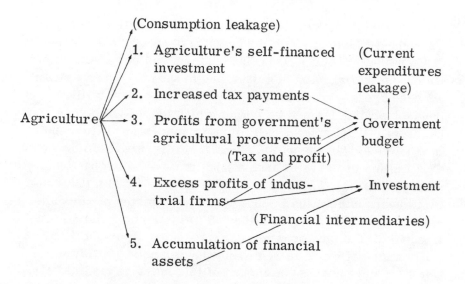

The principal leakages are indicated to emphasize that insofar as income was used for private or public consumption purposes, it would be unavailable for investment.

The influence of land reform in this context can be divided into two broad categories: its impact on agricultural output (and therefore on these flows) and its impact on these flows stemming from the structural reorganization of agriculture rather than from changes in output. As I have indicated in Chapters One and Two, the first of these categories has little bearing on the Chinese case. In order to provide the proper empirical context for analyzing the second, I would like to turn initially to an examination of the provisions of the land reform law and to two case studies. While the case studies are of interest in a number of respects, perhaps the most significant thing they reveal is the great emphasis on the equalization of holdings in the land-redistribution process. This suggests the difficulties the state authorities may have encountered in attempting to turn what had previously taken the form of land rent into a source of investment finance: an increase in the consumption of people who are literally living below the subsistence level (e.g., the chance of poor peasants' raising a particular child to maturity was often less than even) is exceedingly difficult to restrain.

And the more formal analysis of the remainder of this chapter bears out just this expectation: while investment via public saving benefitted substantially from the expropriation, the gains in public saving were limited by the improvements in consumption of the poorer peasants. Agricultural taxation is shown to account for 8% of the gross investment in China in 1952, and profits associated with the margin between the state purchase and sales prices of agricultural commodities are a negligible amount, possibly amounting to 1% of gross investment. The agricultural sector is shown, however, to have made a considerable contribution to saving through its purchase of industrial products at prices higher than those that would have prevailed under competitive conditions, i.e., via manipulation of the terms of trade between agricultural and nonagricultural commodities, the difference taking the form of increasing the funds available for direct investment by industrial enterprises or of increasing their contribution to state investment via their profit (where publicly owned) and tax contribution to the state budget. As will be spelled out in greater detail below, and as has been argued in Chapter One, the land reform played the central role in making this manipulation of the intersectoral terms of trade possible.

The Agrarian Reform
Law of 1950

The primary objectives of the Agrarian Reform Law (5),
enumerated in Article 1, were the elimination of the feudal
landlord system and the development of agricultural production.
The latter was seen as a precondition for the country's industrialization. The act placed great emphasis on the equalization
of holdings, although perfect equality was neither sought nor
obtained. Since the development of production was one of its
primary objectives, it sought as far as possible to distinguish
between "feudal" property and industrial and commercial capital, specifically exempting the latter from expropriation. As
is clear from the wording of the act and from its implementation, "feudal" property and practices were meant to include
those in which the contribution to production of the owner of
land or capital (but not the land or capital in itself) was nil;
while commercial and industrial capital and practices were
meant to include those in which the owner of the capital made
a clear-cut entrepreneurial or managerial contribution to production, distinct from and in addition to the services of the
capital itself. Needless to say, the distinction between feudal
and industrial-commercial activities was in practice frequently
impossible to draw clearly. Lending at usurious rates of interest was sharply restricted as a feudal practice, for example.
The effect of these restrictions spilled over into production,
however, as they led to a further tightening of the usually
severe shortage of agricultural credit.

Nevertheless, without the active awareness of the importance
of managerial and entrepreneurial services on the part of the
government and its attempt to preserve them as far as possible,
it is unlikely that agricultural production could have recovered
so rapidly from the depressed levels of the postwar period. (6)
Also consistent with this outlook is the fact that the land was
not nationalized. (7)

In accordance with the above discussion, Articles 2 and 3 of
the Reform Law call for the requisitioning of "the land, draught

animals, farm implements and surplus grains of the landlords, and their surplus houses in the countryside," as well as "the rural land belonging to ancestral shrines, temples, monasteries, churches, schools and organizations, and other land owned by public bodies," charging local government with the task of providing for the maintenance of these institutions. At the same time, Article 4 states in strong and unambiguous terms:

> Industrial and commercial enterprises operated by landlords and the land and other properties used by landlords directly for the operation of industrial and commercial enterprises shall not be confiscated. In confiscating feudal land and other properties, no infringement upon industry and commerce shall be permitted.

People who held other jobs (such as peddlers, soldiers, professional people, etc.) and families lacking labor power (old couples, widows, orphans, etc.) were allowed to retain land they rented up to a maximum of 200% of the average per capita holding in the locality per family member. Land owned by rich peasants and cultivated by themselves or — within limits — hired labor, together with their other properties (including rented land of no greater area than that tilled by themselves) were to be protected from infringement. It should be noted, however, that prior policy toward rich peasants was more ambiguous, that redistribution was carried out by peasant associations composed of poor and middle peasants (with the former dominating), and that the pressures to increase the properties available for redistribution were enormous. Under these circumstances the measures to protect the property rights of rich peasants were often ignored. Middle peasants were generally not strongly affected by the redistribution, with the most notable exceptions occurring when such families had collaborated with the Japanese occupation.

The land taken was to be redistributed to the poor and landless peasants in an attempt to equalize holdings as far as

possible on a per capita basis. Landlords were to receive an
equal share, as were those clergymen willing and able to do
agricultural work. As far as possible, land was to go to the
present tiller. Other properties were to be similarly distributed. The large farms and plantations (few in number) which
were organized on a capitalist basis (using machinery, under
centralized management, and so forth) were to be kept intact
and the management retained, although they were subject to
nationalization where owned by landlords.

The land reform law was followed by a series of measures
clarifying the definition of class status. These measures am-
plified on earlier ones which had guided the land reform process
prior to 1949. The class status of each individual in each village was determined by the local peasant association on the
basis of whether or not he engaged in labor, what proportion of
his income was from exploitation (renting land, hiring labor,
and usury), and his standard of living. There were many marginal cases extremely difficult to determine, and undoubtedly a
fair number of errors were made. The overall impact of the
land reform was, however, far from ambiguous. It resulted in
a great diminution in the inequality of income and property ownership which had existed in rural China. The impact of this
equalization on the national savings-investment ratio I shall
trace out below. First, however, a review of the two most
authoritative firsthand investigations of the implementation of
the land reform can help to clarify further what actually took
place.

Two case
studies

The two most detailed accounts of the land reform appear in
William Hinton's Fanshen and in C. K. Yang's A Chinese Village
in Early Communist Transition. (8) Both are eyewitness accounts by sophisticated observers who collected their data carefully. In many respects, moreover, the studies complement one

another: Hinton's study is of the village of Changchuang in Shansi Province in north China; Yang's study is of the village of Nanching in Kwangtung Province in south China, five miles from the city of Canton. Changchuang was near no urban center of comparable size. The land reform there took place prior to 1949, while that in Nanching did not take place until after the establishment of the People's Republic.

Among the 251 families of Changchuang, the land redistribution took the form shown in Table 3-1. Several facts stand out clearly from this tabulation. First, it can be seen that landlords held only 12.1% of the land directly before liberation, that there was only one pure tenant family in the village, and that small holders or middle peasants constituted some 40% of the population. (9) The picture which emerges is very much in accord with the data presented in Buck's studies of north China, and it is apparent that the concentration of landholding was not at all extreme and that pure tenancy was uncommon. If we add to these features the extreme poverty of the community as a whole, it would scarcely seem to offer auspicious conditions for the redistribution of land and other property. This, however, is precisely what makes it such a revealing case study.

Concealed beneath the aggregate data lay sharp differences in individual circumstances. Since the people of this village lay so close to the physical margin of subsistence, with the income of the middle peasants barely adequate to sustain life, there was a great difference between those who fell below this mark and those who exceeded it. Rich peasants and landlords, moreover, typically supplemented their income through high-interest loans, control of institutional land, and control of local government, among other means. (10) Their control of institutional land helps to clarify the reason why such land was included in the land reform. (11)

Several other facts brought out by Hinton's study are of particular interest. The land owned by the Catholic Church in the village was rented at the going rates, generally under 50% of the yield but sometimes reaching that level; but there was a

Table 3-1

Land Redistribution in the Village of Changchuang,
Lucheng County, Shansi Province

	Number of families	% of families	Number of persons	% of population	Land held (mou*)	% of land held	Mou* per capita	
I. Before liberation								
Landlord	7	2.8	39	4	680	12.1	17.4	
Rich peasant	5	2	27	2.7	303	5.4	11.2	
Middle peasant	81	32.2	395	40	2,532.6	45.3	6.4	
Poor peasant	138	55	462	46.8	1,386.4	24.8	3	
Hired laborer	19	7.6	59	6	—	—	—	
Tenant	1	.4	5	.5	—	—	—	
Institutional	—	—	—	—	686.2	13.3	—	
Totals	251	100	987	100	5,588.2	100		
								Change (in mou*)
II. Between liberation and May 4, 1946								
Landlord	2	.8	6	.6	18	.3	3	−662
Rich peasant	4	1.6	20	2.1	138.8	2.5	6.9	−164.2
Middle peasant	76	31.2	349	37.4	2,157	38.6	6.2	−375.6
Poor peasant	162	66.4	559	59.9	2,841.4	50.8	5	+1,455
Institutional	—	—	—	—	433	7.8	—	−253.2
Totals	244	100	934	100	5,588.2	100		

	Number of families	% of families	Number of persons	% of population	Land held (mou*)	% of land held	Mou* per capita	Change (in mou*)
III. After completion of May 4 Movement (1946)								
Landlord	1	.4	2	.2	18	.3	9	0
Rich peasant	4	1.6	12	1.3	82.6	1.5	6.9	−56.2
Middle peasant	76	30.4	338	35.5	2,095	37.5	6.2	−62
Poor peasant	169	67.6	599	63	3,309.6	59.2	5.5	+468.2
Institutional	—	—	—	—	83	1.5	—	−350
Totals	250	100	951	100	5,588.2	100		

IV. After 1948 movement

	Number of families	% of families	Number of persons	% of population	Land held (mou*)	% of land held	Mou* per capita	Change (in mou*)
Landlord	1	.4	2	.2	13.5	.2	6.7	−4.5
Rich peasant	4	1.6	12	1.3	55.5	1	4.6	−27.1
Old middle peasant	76	30.4	341	35.5	2,056.6	36.6	6	−38.4
New middle peasant	140	56	523	54.5	3,048.3	54.2	5.8	+67
Poor peasant	29	11.6	82	8.5	415.8	7.4	5.1	+87.5
Institutional	—	—	—	—	36	.6	—	−47
Totals	250	100	960	100	5,625.7†	100		

Source: William Hinton, Fanshen, p. 592.

Notes:

*Six mou equals one acre.

†Reclaimed land and land administratively transferred from other villages account for the increase in total land after the 1948 movement.

modest deduction of one-eighth for land rented to Catholics. In
general, institutional land was rented at going rates throughout
China, although there were a number of instances in which members received reduced rates when membership was not large in
relation to the wealth of the institution. Also of interest is the
fact that the rich peasants too were by and large expropriated,
despite higher-level attempts to restrain this process. In the
case of Changchuang, some of the middle peasants were also
expropriated in whole or in part, both because of their relative
wealth and more importantly because of their collaboration with
the Japanese occupation army.

Before the land reform the landlords and rich peasants constituted 7% of the population and owned 164 acres, or 18% of the
land, and 33% of the draft animals. (12) Through religious and
clan associations they controlled another 114 acres, so that the
land under their control altogether came to some 31% of the
land area. The middle peasants, comprising 40% of the population, held 45% of the land and 66% of the draft animals. The
poor peasants comprised 47% of the population and held 24% of
the land. (13) Hired laborers comprised 6% of the population.
The land reform took place in several stages. By the time it
ended, some 340 acres (14), or 36% of the land, had been redistributed to the poor and landless peasants in a village where
landlords had held only 12.1% of the land. (15) Rich-peasant
land and institutional land, together with a fair amount of richer-
middle-peasant land, accounted for the difference. Those families with a roof over their heads and approximately the average
per capita holding of land were reclassified as "new middle
peasants." This case study demonstrates the emphasis on
equality of holdings in the land-redistribution process and helps
to clarify the reasons why the amount of land redistributed in
the course of the land reform throughout China, 44% of the total
arable land, was so much in excess of the 33.5% (16) farmed by
tenants in China. It has also been estimated that 3-5% of the
land area was owned by small land lessors who were unaffected
by the reform (17), so that the tenanted land available for

redistribution would have amounted only to about 30% of the total arable land area, or a shade over two-thirds of the redistributed land. Further insight into the actual process of the land reform is provided by C. K. Yang's study of Nanching in south China.

Nanching is about five miles from the city of Canton. Thus, although its agrarian character was preserved at least until the early 1950s, in various respects its proximity to a major metropolis made it somewhat atypical of rural China in general. Nevertheless, where "distortions" appear, their direction can generally be unambiguously ascertained; and since the compilation of the data was quite thorough and the observer highly sophisticated, the study of this community, too, represents a major contribution to our understanding of the process of land reform in China.

In 1948 the population of Nanching was about 1,100, and the area of crop land 1,200 mou, or about 200 acres. (18) Thus there was slightly over one mou, or one-sixth of an acre, of land per capita. While the man-land ratio of this village was particularly high due to its location in the Pearl River Delta, one of the most fertile parts of China, it reflects the much smaller availability of land and smaller farm size typical of south China, where much rainfall and a mild climate make multiple cropping feasible. Of the 1,200 mou, 80 mou was clan, temple, and educational land. This 6.2% of the land as institutional land was sometimes substantially exceeded in other parts of south China: 30% of the land of Panyu County, in which Nanching was situated, for example, comprised clan land. Eight hundred and forty mou, including the institutional land, or 70% of Nanching's total land, was rented, while 360 mou, or 30%, was tilled by owners. Five families, or 2.18% of the 230 families, held 310 mou, or 25.8% of the best cultivated land.

The rent was generally 43% of the gross yield and was collected twice a year, right after each harvest (the rent for the much less productive unirrigated land, limited in quantity, was lower). The landlords provided no management or other inputs.

The nonlabor cost of production (borne by the tenant) was about
10% of the gross yield, including 7% for fertilizer and seeds, so
that the tenant paid as rent 43 ÷ 90, or 47.8% of the net yield.
In addition, as noted above in Chapter Two, a rent deposit equal
to half a year's rent was demanded of the tenants. (19) Institutional land was rented out on the same terms as private land,
and "a common complaint against clan ownership of land was
corrupt management in the form of embezzlement of rents and
favoritism in renting good land to well-placed members." (20)

In Nanching, too, middle-peasant status marked the physical
subsistence dividing line. In 1949 the infant mortality rate was
300 per 1,000 births, and the poor considered themselves lucky
if two children could be raised to maturity out of six or seven
live births. The largest landowner held 120 mou, or 10% of the
village land. He had first become wealthy as a member of a
local bandit gang and from opium traffic, and had used the capital thus acquired to establish a legitimate import-export business in Canton. Prior to the land reform he fled to Hong Kong.
His story makes clear the practical difficulty of distinguishing
between "feudal" and capitalist activities when both were embodied in the same person.

In the land reform in Nanching, 460 mou of private land and
the entire 80 mou of institutional land were seized for redistribution. The total 540 mou represented 45% of the village
land. This left 300 mou, or 25% of the village land, in the hands
of small land lessors, versus the national average of 3-5%.
Some of these were families who lacked the requisite labor
power, but the majority constituted the small holdings of city
emigrants who supplemented the small remittances they were
able to send home to their families with the rental income.
This situation was uncommon: the proximity of Nanching to a
major metropolis, and through it to more distant areas, made
it a special case.

Based on a per capita norm of slightly less than one mou and
the number of members in each family, 130 families received
land. Since most of the recipients already held small bits of

land, totalling 80 mou in all, they were to receive enough land
to bring them up to the norm. They included all the 100-odd
poor peasant families, peddlers whose unenvied livelihood was
the product of insufficient land, some returning emigrants, and
the former landlords, who were entitled to their average per
capita share.

The redistribution of land was followed by changes in taxation.
The new tax in the village of Nanching, according to Yang's report, was 30% of the gross yield in the years 1949-1951, versus
the 10% level which had previously prevailed. (21) This (the
former figure) was far in excess of government regulations (22)
and seems to have resulted from the overzealousness of rural
cadres eager to surpass their quotas. (23)

The contribution of agricultural taxation
to the national savings-investment
ratio since the land reform

The discussion of the case studies in the previous section was
meant to clarify the content and processes of the land reform
and ultimately to illuminate the connection between the land reform and the investment-savings changes discussed below. To
further the latter intention, a return to an examination of the
aggregate data is now in order. Table 1 in the Statistical Appendix presents the aggregate data on national income and the
relevant savings-investment amounts and ratios for the years
1933 and 1952-1957. Line 8 of the table reveals the data for
net domestic investment as a percentage of net domestic expenditure. The same table makes it possible to calculate gross
domestic investment as a percentage of gross domestic expenditure. Calculated in terms of constant 1952 prices (except for
1933, whose ratios are calculated in terms of current prices
for the reasons explained below), the percentages are as shown
in Table 3-2.

The Liu and Yeh estimates from which these ratios are derived almost certainly overstate the level of 1933 net domestic

Table 3-2

Gross and Net Investment as a Percentage of Gross
and Net Domestic Expenditure, 1933 and 1952-1957

	1933	1952	1953	1954	1955	1956	1957
$\dfrac{\text{NDI}}{\text{NDE}} \times 100$	1.7	15.4	20.2	21.0	21.6	22.3	21.9
$\dfrac{\text{GDI}}{\text{GDE}} \times 100$	5.0	19.0	23.9	24.8	25.4	26.5	26.2

Source: Statistical Appendix, Table 1.
Notes:
NDI and GDI are net and gross domestic investment respectively. NDE and GDE are net and gross domestic expenditure
respectively.

Calculations for 1933 are in terms of current yuan; for the
other years they are in terms of constant 1952 yuan.

investment in 1952 prices: thus I have indicated the 1933 ratios
calculated in terms of current prices. The method Liu and Yeh
used to estimate 1933 investment in terms of 1952 prices was
to deduct personal consumption, communal services, and government consumption for 1933, all valued in 1952 prices and estimated at 56.53, 0.32, and 2.36 billion yuan, respectively (p. 637),
from their estimate of 61.76 billion yuan for net domestic expenditure in 1933 (also valued in 1952 prices). Thus their investment estimate is a residual. A 1% error in their estimate
for personal consumption alone — and their estimating procedures leave room for a much wider range of error — would
result in a 22% change in their net domestic investment estimate. Moreover, while their index number of 500 for 1933 investment valued in 1952 prices (1933 = 100) is consistent with
the increase in the price of capital goods, investment also includes construction (for which their own value-added index is
304, where 1933 = 100) and additions to inventories, including

raw materials, fuels, goods in the process of production, etc.
(for which the price increase in the aggregate was also less than
for capital goods). Since prices were essentially market determined in 1933, I have included the investment ratios for that
year calculated in current prices.

If calculated in 1933 prices, the investment ratios for the
1950s would appear lower. This is not an especially meaningful
process, however, in light of the objections noted above and because it is my purpose here to measure the share of national
income which went into savings (or investment) in different
years, not to show changes in the level of real investment over
time. Furthermore, in setting prices for producer goods the
government was still following market forces in 1952 — and the
effect of economic reconstruction, the U.S. embargo, and the
Korean War was to push up these prices relative to others. (24)
The high investment ratios during this period cannot, accordingly, be viewed as a consequence of simple overvaluation of
investment goods. (25)

Nineteen fifty-two is the first year after 1949 for which comprehensive national income data are available; and since it also
marks the terminal year of the land reform, most of my re-
marks will be concerned with the 1952 data. The data on accumulation for subsequent years show that after a further jump
in 1953 over the (already) high accumulation ratio of 1952,
bringing the net ratio to 20.2% of net domestic expenditure,
further percentage increases were quite modest. This suggests
that in seeking to assess the impact of institutional change on
the increase in the investment ratio, the period up to 1952-1953
is of greatest importance.

In 1952 state revenue came to 17,560 million yuan. (26) (The
state budget "comprises the revenues and expenditures of both
the central government and all levels of local government." [27])
Of this revenue, 7,630 million yuan (28), or 43% of the total,
went into economic construction: investment in basic construction and working capital. (29) Investment financed through the
state budget, therefore, was 68% of the 11.26 billion yuan net

domestic investment, or 53% of the 14.52 billion yuan gross
domestic investment in 1952. (30) Agricultural taxation contributed 2,704 million yuan, or 15% of the total budget revenues. (31) If we regard the agricultural taxation revenues as
being divided between investment and public consumption in
the same proportion as budget expenditures as a whole, then
43% of the agricultural taxes collected, or 1,163 million yuan,
may be regarded as having served to finance investment. Thus
1.16 ÷ 14.5 (or 0.15 × 0.53) of the gross investment in the country was financed from agricultural taxation, equal to some
8.0% of the gross investment in 1952. Similarly, agricultural
taxation may be regarded as having financed 10.3% of the net
investment in that year. (32)

The meaning of these figures emerges more distinctly if they
are compared with the situation in the 1930s, when the overall
level of capital formation was small and the government contribution to investment insignificant, so that the contribution of
agricultural taxation to capital formation was negligible. In the
earlier period, the land-tax revenues were completely in the
hands of the provincial and local governments, while the leakages due to tax farming, corruption, and nonregistration of land
were considerable. In view of these considerations, the contribution of agricultural taxation to capital formation in 1952
can be seen to reflect two basic factors: the increase in tax
rates and the tightening of administration — both made possible
by the termination of landlord political authority and claims on
product in rural China brought about by the land reform.

I have indicated in Chapter Two that land taxes would have
reached 1,376 million (old) yuan in 1933 had they been paid on
all land. Since about one-third of the farm land remained unregistered, however, the tax level would have reached 917 million yuan (or 4.3% of the gross agricultural output in that
year [33]). This figure does not include some of the multitudinous surtaxes, local taxes, and special levies described in
Chapter Two; it also fails to take account of the innumerable
leakages noted there, and so represents a thoroughgoing

overstatement of the funds available to the county and provincial governments, which in fact received only about 10% of this amount (34) (the entire agricultural tax went to these local governments until 1940). The tax payments in 1952, on the other hand, went to the central government with sharply reduced leakages and reflect the elimination of most of the extra levies.

It is of course true that higher tax rates might, in theory, have been imposed in the 1930s, but this would have directly affected the interests of the landlord class on whose support the government relied to maintain local government and order and to collect the taxes. Under the pressure of World War II, the government did in fact centralize tax collections and increase the rates, if we regard the forced grain "loans" of the time as a form of taxation. The experience in this regard, however, is also instructive. The maximum collected reached 8.8% of the gross yield of rice and 5.9% of the gross yield of wheat in free China. (35) The government had to employ 200,000 people in the collection process alone. (36) Much of the extra burden was passed on to the tenants (37); this was reflected in sharp wartime rent increases, which were especially severe in Szechwan Province.

The contribution of the agricultural sector to national savings and investment through the increase in tax rates and the stricter tax administration which were made possible by the land reform is clear-cut in nature: it amounted to 8.0% and 10.3% of gross and net domestic saving, respectively, in 1952. Before examining the impact of changes in the urban-rural terms of trade, one more form of direct contribution, self-investment in agriculture, remains to be considered.

Self-investment in agriculture

As I have noted previously, landlords did not typically play an active role in farm management. While farm buildings were often supplied, the expenses for fertilizer, seeds, tools, and so forth were typically borne by the tenant. The high rent charges and marginal living standards of most tenants, together with the high interest rates and the need to offer security for loans on the part of those who lacked property, served as sharp constraints to rural investment in traditional China. These factors curtailed the poor peasants' ability to invest. Their willingness to invest was further curtailed by the necessity not only of bearing the full cost but also of paying a high proportion of the benefits to the landlord, who would also be the beneficiary of permanent improvement in the land. As might be expected, therefore, the land reform, which brought the majority of poor and landless peasants up to or near the status of middle peasants, tended to stimulate self-investment in agriculture. Since one basic purpose of the land reform was to increase production and productivity in agriculture, the local cadres gave great encouragement to this tendency. Moreover, the government tax rates were based on a "normal" yield which was to be reassessed only every three years, so that intervening production increases were not subject to taxation.

Alexander Eckstein estimates that (in 1952)

total self-financed capital formation in agriculture would be Y1,620 million. This would constitute a 5.4% rate of gross capital formation in relation to gross agricultural product, and 4.3% in relation to total farm product. These figures are in keeping with the 3% net rates given in Chinese Communist studies of national income. (38)

These figures suggest that self-financed investment in agriculture was of no little importance. The problems of valuation and estimation are substantial, however, and since any estimates of this sort are necessarily conjectural, self-investment in agriculture is not included in the 14.52 billion yuan gross investment figure cited above. The exclusion of self-investment in agriculture generally produces a downward bias in investment estimates for underdeveloped countries, although not necessarily

in investment ratios, since rural consumption in kind is often
understated as well. Thus the increase in self-investment taking place within agriculture, although likely to have been significant in its contribution to real capital formation, does not
enter into the changes in the investment ratios that I have been
seeking to explain. The importance of this omission is indicated
by comparison with the 1930s when, as indicated in Chapter Two,
net capital formation in agriculture may have been nil. Since
the agricultural sector contributed 48% to national income in
1952 (39), a 3% rate of net capital formation would amount to
1.4% of net domestic product in that year.

The indirect contribution
of the agricultural sector to the
national savings-investment ratio

In considering the indirect contributions to investment of the
agricultural sector, both the state purchases at low prices of
agricultural produce and the profits and taxes on sales of goods
to the rural sector by the industrial sector must be taken into
account. Both of these elements are reflected in the terms of
trade between the agricultural and industrial sectors. A look
at the change in the terms of trade will help to clarify the issues
involved. Parts A and B of Table 8 in the Statistical Appendix
provide the relevant information concerning the terms of trade.
They show that between 1930 and 1933 the terms of trade turned
sharply against the agricultural sector and that the relationship
between industrial and agricultural prices in 1952 was adverse
to agriculture compared to the 1930-1936 period. From 1950,
however, there was steady improvement from the standpoint of
peasant producers, as government procurement prices rose
while the cost of manufactured goods remained roughly constant; this shift was to continue into the 1960s, when it was accelerated by the lower prices set for agricultural producer
goods.
While these changes in the terms of trade are of historical

interest, they do not in themselves demonstrate price distortion; secular shifts in relative production costs and the organization of economic activity would have brought changes in relative prices even in the absence of conscious price manipulation. Furthermore, the comparison between the early 1930s and the early 1950s is especially difficult to undertake, because in the former period China's currency was tied to a silver standard. World silver prices, like those of other minerals, dropped sharply with the onset of the Great Depression but then rose sharply with the passage of the Silver Purchase Act of 1932 in the United States (40); China's prices moved inversely. Agricultural prices seem to have been especially hard hit by the domestic deflation which rising world silver prices created (see Table 8 Part A in the Statistical Appendix). These considerations, while not ruling out the possibility of using historical shifts in the terms of trade in making intertemporal comparisons of peasant welfare, indicate the impracticality of using such shifts in themselves to measure the degree of price manipulation.

In fact, there is no entirely unambiguous means of measuring the degree of price manipulation in a case like this, because it is necessary to compare actual prices with those that would have prevailed in the absence of the government's economic role, and this in turn depends on the assumptions one makes concerning market structure and so forth. The standard against which I measure actual price performance below in evaluating the government's control over the terms of trade implies a fair degree of competition, with a 10% rate of return on industrial sales, including the distributive margin. One could, with equal plausibility, assume a more oligopolistic market structure, under which prices would have been higher (and compared with which actual prices would appear to show less distortion). The advantage of making the more competitive assumption lies in its calling attention to the major distributive question that arises in connection with the government's policy of maintaining high prices and reaping high profits (and taxes) from the

sale of industrial products in the countryside: how could the
government, brought to power by an agrarian revolution and
still finding its essential support in the countryside, sustain
terms of trade so adverse to its partisans? Further, how could
it do so without negatively affecting agricultural incentives, productivity, and willingness to market output?

These questions can best be considered by first measuring
the magnitude of resources extracted from the agricultural sector by adverse terms of trade, and this in turn can best be done
within the framework provided by equation (10) on page 19 of
Chapter One, which is reproduced below:

$$B_a \quad = \frac{(P_m - P_x)}{P_x} hQ + \frac{(P_i - P_j)}{P_i} V \tag{10}$$

By measuring the extent to which actual prices received and
paid by farmers deviated from the prices which would have been
established under competitive market conditions, the impact of
the rural-industrial terms of trade on the flow of resources
from agriculture to industrial enterprises and then into investment (typically via the government budget) can be ascertained.
High prices for industrial goods swelled the profits and taxes
of the sellers, thereby making possible an increase in investment (see the discussion and diagram on pages 95-96).

Information on profit rates in light industry and on retail
sales in rural areas helps to provide the basis for a rough estimate of the role of the terms of trade between industry and
agriculture in contributing to capital formation. The average
pretax profit rate of light industry in the 1950s was 32% of cost,
and that of commerce 11%. (41) Adding the two gives a rough
estimate of tax plus profit as a percent of average cost:
.32 + .11(1.32) = .47, or 47%. Suppose a 10% rate of return
on sales, a rate within which the distributor's return is included,
would prevail under modestly imperfect competitive conditions. (42) Then peasant purchasers paid 34% more than the
"competitive" cost of production, including the return to capital.
Alternatively stated, roughly 25% of the prices paid by peasants

for industrial products represented "surplus profits," and this portion of sales constitutes a contribution — made by agriculture's adverse terms of trade — to increasing the national savings ratio. It is of interest to note that according to official price estimates, the terms of trade in 1952 were 22% more adverse to agriculture than in the 1930-1936 period. (43)

Thus $(P_i - P_j)/P_i$ is .25, and one-fourth of the retail sales of goods in villages can be treated as an exaction from the rural populace for the purpose of financing an expansion of investment. The level of rural retail sales appears in Table 3-3. Twenty-five percent of the 15.52 billion yuan of rural retail sales (this is V in equation [10]) in 1952 is 3.88 billion yuan. This constitutes 26.7% of the 14.52 billion yuan gross investment in that year, or 34.5% of the 11.26 billion yuan net investment. These percentages may be regarded as the rural sector's contribution to the capital formation financed by the industrial taxes and excess profits associated with the adverse terms of trade.

Table 3-3

Rural Retail Sales as a Proportion of Total Retail Sales
(in billions of current yuan)

Year	A Amount of retail sales of goods in villages	B Total retail sales in society	A as % of B
1950		17.06	
1952	15.52	27.68	56
1953	18.38	34.80	53
1954	20.83	38.11	55
1955	25.60	39.22	65
1956	28.27	46.10	61
1957		47.42	
1958		54.80	

Source: Shigeru Ishikawa, National Income and Capital Formation in Mainland China, pp. 177 and 180.

This discussion of the magnitudes involved provides the proper setting for consideration of the questions raised at the outset: how could the regime, dependent on rural support, sustain such high prices without alienating its support and causing a fall in production and marketing incentives? Its capacity to do so can be ascribed to two principal factors. First, with the hyperinflation and economic collapse which marked the closing years of the Kuomintang regime, much of the intersectoral trade had been curtailed, so that the new conditions are apt to have been perceived as less adverse than they actually were. Second, and of far greater importance, the redistribution of income associated with the land reform made even adverse terms of trade compatible with a higher standard of living on the part of the majority of the peasantry, as the discussion below will demonstrate — and the new terms are not apt to have been perceived as particularly adverse by those who previously had little to trade.

Thus changes in the terms of trade between agriculture and industry, changes which the new regime could sustain because of the redistribution of income which attended the land reform, had a part to play in contributing to the increase in capital formation in China. But inflated purchase prices are only one part of the terms of trade picture. The prices received for agricultural products must also be considered.

In 1953 the government stocks of food proved inadequate to meet demand. The resulting crisis led to the government decision in November 1953 to institute the system of the "planned purchase and planned supply" of grain, according to which peasants were to sell grain to the state in quantities fixed by and at prices determined by the government. (44) Prior to this time, grain prices were, for the most part, market determined. A more elaborate set of requirements, the "three fix" policy, was adopted in 1955, under which fixed production quotas were set for compulsory sales to the state and fixed sales levels established for state grain supplies which were sold to grain-deficient peasants. From the production quota fixed on the land

owned by each household or cooperative, consumption, animal
fodder, and seed requirements were deducted, and 80-90% of
the remaining surplus had to be sold to the state. (45) What is
of chief interest concerning these measures is the fact that they
were adopted after the sharp increases in the national savings
ratio had taken place. Thus government monopsony power in
grain purchases cannot have been a significant factor in accounting for this increase in the savings ratio.

While many of the new Chinese institutions were modeled on
those developed in the Soviet Union, the high turnover tax on
agricultural products of the latter was not adopted in China. (46)
"The Minister of Food, Sha Ch'ien-li, writing in October 1959,
stated that purchasing and retailing prices of grains were based
on the free market prices of 1953." (47) If so — and there is
no reason to presume the minister's information incorrect —
the manipulation of such prices could not have played a major
role in financing investment. Citing the same source (48),
Donnithorne writes:

> According to the Minister of Food in 1959, the margin be-
> tween the purchase and sales prices of grains in rural areas
> had been stabilized at about 8% (whether 8% of the purchase
> or of the sales price is not stated); this included manage-
> ment expenses and a small element of tax. However, the
> industrial and commercial tax on grain had, in 1958, been
> fixed at 4% of the purchasing price (i.e., it would account
> for half the margin of 8%). In the spring of 1958 the margin
> on grain was described as having been "exceedingly small"
> in the previous few years. Indeed it was stated that before
> the autumn of 1955 a loss had in fact usually been incurred.
> The management expenses which the Minister of Food
> mentioned as being met out of the 8% margin on grain prices
> in rural areas presumably referred only to trading costs,
> not to the cost of processing the grain. (49)

According to the budget plan for 1959, the only year for

which sufficient data for this calculation are available,

> the target for commercial profits from grain was around
> Y400 million...and the target for profits on the processing
> of grain was Y130 million.... This compares with a total
> of Y3,300 million for revenue from the agricultural tax in
> the budget for 1959. Thus agricultural tax was budgeted to
> provide over eight times as much revenue as did commer-
> cial profit on grain.... (50)

Thus if the same proportion had held for 1952, when agricultural taxation contributed 8% of gross investment, commercial
profits on state grain procurement and sales would have contributed a negligible 1%. In fact, as it is revealed that prior
to 1955 losses were generally incurred on the sale of grain in
rural areas, the actual contribution when urban areas are included may have been still less than 1%.

While reliable data on grain output and government procurement for 1952 are not available, the figures for 1953, indicating
that 27% of total grain output went through government hands in
that year (see Table 3-4), before the planned purchase and supply went into effect, may reflect the general situation in 1952.

Table 3-4

Total Grain Output and Government Collection
(data in million metric tons)

	Total output of grain	Grain paid in tax	State pur- chase of grain	Total state collection	Procurement as % of total output
1953	157	20	23	43	27
1954	160	22	32	54	34

Source: Audrey Donnithorne, China's Economic System, p. 357.
Note: Government purchases until late 1953 were on the open
market, after which quota requirements and forced sales were
instituted.

In addition, it is known that "between 1953-1957 the state had acquired by tax and purchase 28% of the total grain output of these years. After deducting grain sold in rural areas, net retention was 16.5% of total output." (51) Thus it can be seen that while much of the grain was returned to rural areas, a very substantial portion of the total passed through the hands of the state trading agencies responsible for supplying the cities. The state's high degree of control over supplies, however, was not used directly as a major source of government or investment finance. (52)

This information is in accord with the investment estimates indicated above, which showed that the sharpest increases in the national savings-investment ratio had by and large been realized by 1953, whereas the tightening of government grain control following the decree of November 1953, when it was undertaken to ensure the availability of supplies rather than as a revenue measure, did not really take effect until 1954. Thus, although the government's nontax procurement of agricultural produce became substantial after the installment of the new regime in 1949, its procurement activities made no appreciable contribution to development finance.

The impact on output

Other historically unique changes and conditions accompanied the land reform in China, making it difficult to isolate the specific impact of land reform on output. Even so, sufficient evidence is present to justify several broad assertions. One can say with confidence that the land reform was entirely compatible with a rapid recovery from the depressed levels of output that accompanied the wartime and civil war conditions. Official Chinese sources indicate that at the start of 1950 agricultural production had fallen to two-thirds of the prewar level and that the share of output marketed was down to 17% (from over 25%). (53) The first estimate is almost certainly an exaggeration, and the second may well be too, although it is not inconsistent with the chaotic trade conditions which accompanied the postwar hyperinflation. Still, it is clear that production was down, and that the 1950-1952 period witnessed a healthy recovery. (54)

The relation of the land reform to this recovery is not hard to explain. Landlords did not typically provide management services or furnish essential inputs (other than land), so their disappearance cannot have hurt production. Rural credit conditions became tighter than they had been, but credit had never been plentiful and most had found its way into nonproductive uses. The disappearance of banditry and the motley army of nonproductive individuals who lived off the peasantry can only have been beneficial. Yet despite these changes, the basic production organization of Chinese agriculture remained the same (55): many small, individual producers working scattered strips of land with a technology that had been little changed since the tenth century. (56) The availability of inputs, moreover, remained roughly the same.

The redistribution of land may have provided some additional production incentive to peasant producers, but this can have been only marginal at best. This stems from the fact that even though the tenant had had to give up close to half of his net output to the landlord, his income was too low to permit this to manifest itself in a reduced work effort: he had to work as hard as he could, within the confines set by the available capital equipment and technology, just to live, and so could work no harder when the redistribution of land raised the share of his marginal product he could retain. Over the relevent range the supply curve of labor was roughly vertical, rather than sloping up to the right. Only the reorganization of farming associated with the collectivization which followed could substantially increase the labor input in agricultural production. (57)

Thus the contribution of the land reform to increasing production cannot have been outstanding, despite the removal of nonproductive individuals from the scene (or their transformation into producers). (58) The land reform was consistent with the recovery in production and helped it along; but without basic changes in the organization of agricultural activity, technology, or production inputs, it was incapable of bringing about a rapid increase in output. This limitation of the land reform in increasing output was reflected in the decision to accelerate the planned pace of collectivization, a subject on which I shall touch in the next chapter.

Summary

The scope of the land reform in China was substantial. It involved the transfer of 700 million mou of land, or 44% of China's arable land area. Despite the redistribution of land, the system of private ownership was retained. Thus the organization of agricultural activity remained essentially the same; and with the technology and level of inputs also unchanged, the land reform proved capable of facilitating recovery in the depressed rural sector, but not, in itself, of providing the basis for a rapid expansion in agricultural productivity and output once recovery had been made.

It is, then, primarily the redistributive effects of the land reform which account for its contribution to raising the national savings ratio. In terms of the analytic schema proposed in Chapter One*, income streams flowing into classes 1 and 2 were diverted, in the first instance, to class 3, producers of subsistence (nonluxury) goods and services: to the peasant producers of food. In turn, a portion of this gain was extracted through taxation and a portion extracted by maintaining terms of trade adverse to agriculture in its exchange relations with the industrial sector; both of these extracted shares helped to finance an expansion in employment and output in class 4, composed of the producers of capital goods. Taxation of the agricultural sector accounted for 8.0% and 10.3% of gross and net

*See p. 21.

capital formation in 1952. Manipulation of the terms of trade,
primarily through pricing industrial products substantially
above cost, extracted an additional amount from the agricultural sector, constituting 26.7% and 34.5% of gross and net investment, respectively. The land reform, therefore, can be
said to account for 5.04 billion yuan of 1952 investment (59):
this is 44.8% of the 11.26 billion yuan net investment, or 34.7%
of the 14.52 billion yuan gross investment in that year.

Net domestic product in 1952 was 71.41 billion yuan. (60)
Net value added in agriculture in that year was 34.19 billion
yuan. (61) If interest payments remained the same 2.8% of national income they were in 1933, and if rent and the value
added by full-time hired labor remained the same 16.4% and
5.2%, respectively, of value added in the agricultural sector (62),
then interest payments in 1952 would have come to 2.00 billion
yuan; the value added by hired peasants would have come to
1.78 billion yuan more than their income; and land rent would
have come to 5.61 billion yuan. These three together, totaling
9.39 billion yuan, represent gains to the poor and landless
peasants which land reform made possible. The gains would
be higher if the savings from the elimination of banditry, tax
farming, and so forth, which are not precisely quantifiable,
were included. The 5.04 billion yuan in savings extracted from
the agricultural sector through taxation and control over the
terms of trade with the industrial sector may be measured
against this more than 9.39 billion yuan gain from the land
reform.

Thus land reform brought an increase of more than 9.39
billion yuan to those in class 3, of which the government was
able to extract 5.04 billion yuan for increasing employment
and output in class 4 — in the capital goods sector of the economy. (Total extractions were somewhat greater than this, as
the discussion below will make clear, because part of the agricultural tax revenues were used for public consumption rather
than capital formation.) The land reform was capable of enabling the agricultural sector to make a substantial, if not majority,

contribution to capital formation in 1952. Government policy was successful in withdrawing some of the benefits of institutional change from their recipients, but the high marginal income elasticity of demand for food and other necessities on the part of the poor peasants, as well as the government's desire to retain their support and improve their living standards, put limits on the portion of the gain which could be extracted. As a consequence, the land reform brought both higher real incomes to most of China's peasantry and an increase in the national savings ratio.

This impact of the land reform can be further clarified by referring back to equations (7-10) on page 19 of Chapter One. The equations are reproduced below for ready reference:

$$\Delta Y_p = rQ + r'Q + iL_{tp} = \Delta C_p + \Delta S_p + \Delta M_p \qquad (7)$$
$$\Delta M_p = \Delta T_a + \Delta B_a \qquad (8)$$
$$T_a = nQ \qquad (9)$$
$$B_a = \frac{(P_m - P_x)}{P_x} hQ + \frac{(P_i - P_j)}{P_i} V \qquad (10)$$

Since price manipulation was not significant with regard to the state purchase of agricultural products, P_x was approximately equal to P_m, $P_m - P_x = 0$, and the first term on the right side of equation (10) becomes zero. B_a, the gain from the manipulation of the terms of trade between industry and agriculture, depends entirely on the second term then, which represents the revenue gains to the state and, to a lesser extent, to private firms from selling industrial products in the countryside at "inflated" prices. $(P_i - P_j)/P_i$ has been estimated at 0.25 and V at 15.52 billion yuan. B_a, therefore, is 0.25(15.52 billion yuan), or 3.88 billion yuan. Since control over the terms of trade played no significant role in capital formation prior to the revolution, ΔB_a is also 3.88 billion yuan.

T_a was shown to be 2.70 billion yuan. The 917 million yuan paid in agricultural taxes in 1933 (see Chapter Two) would have been worth 1.66 billion yuan in 1952 prices. (63) Of the 1.66

billion yuan, one-third had been paid by landlords, two-thirds by peasants (as land farmed by tenants was one-third of the total). Thus 1.10 billion yuan (taxes owner-farmers would presumably have paid in the absence of land reform) must be subtracted from the 2.70 billion yuan to get ΔT_a, which is therefore equal to 1.60 billion yuan. ΔM_p, accordingly, is 5.48 billion yuan.

ΔY_p, the income of rural property owners prior to the land reform and incremental peasant income after it, was found in Chapter Two to be 16.9% of national income. Between 1950 and 1952, however, the growth of the economy reduced the share of agricultural value added in national income, so that the initial gains to the poor and landless peasants amounted to 13.1% of 1952's 71.41 billion yuan net domestic product (64), the 9.39 billion yuan indicated above. This figure, however, understates the real gain, as it does not include the gains accruing to the peasants as a consequence of the abolition of the multitudinous illegal and semilegal exactions (discussed in Chapter Two) which the land reform brought about. Since ΔY_p is 9.39 billion yuan and ΔM_p is 5.48 billion yuan, the increase in peasant disposable income for which the land reform is responsible, $\Delta C_p + \Delta S_p$, is 3.91 billion yuan. For the reason just indicated, this figure also understates the real improvement.

In evaluating the contribution of these changes to raising the national savings-investment ratio, I have used the following assumptions. ΔB_a I have treated as a pure gain in saving. (65) My treatment of the contribution of the agricultural tax, on the other hand, is more complex. In the traditional economy, agricultural taxes stayed within the rural sector (and the greater part of them can be treated most reasonably as representing collective consumption on the part of the property-owning classes). They were not available to the central government and made no contribution to the financing of investment. The land reform, breaking the power of the property-owning classes in the countryside, made all tax payments potentially available to finance investment. Thus I have treated the entire post-land-reform agricultural tax receipts, 2.70 billion yuan, in this way — not just ΔT_a. Then, however, I assumed that these receipts were divided between public consumption and public investment in the same proportion as budgetary revenues as a whole. Since 43% of the budget served to finance investment, I have treated the corresponding contribution of agricultural taxation as 0.43 × 2.70 billion yuan, or 1.16 billion yuan. Regarded in this way, the manipulation of urban-rural terms of trade contributed 3.88 billion yuan and agricultural taxation 1.16 billion yuan to 1952's net domestic investment of 11.26 billion yuan and gross domestic investment of 14.52 billion yuan. Thus the land reform, by making these contributions possible, is responsible for 44.8% of the net investment, or 34.7% of the gross investment, which took place in 1952.

Notes

1) Po Yi-po, "Three Years of Achievements of the People's Republic of China," in New China's Economic Achievements, 1949-52, comp. China Committee for the Promotion of International Trade (Peking, 1952), pp. 151-52. One hectare = 2.47 acres.

2) Akira Doi, "The Present Situation of Agricultural Collectivization in China," Asian Affairs, II (March 1957), 50. Since there were some 113,680,000 farm households in 1952, the land per farm household averaged only 0.95 hectares.

3) There are approximately 6 mou to an acre, 15 mou to a hectare.

4) Liao Lu-yen, "The Great Victory in Land Reform During the Past Three Years," in New China's Economic Achievements, 1949-52, p. 171. As Mr. Liao does not cite the assumptions underlying his estimate, it cannot be used to check the estimates in Chapter Two. The following observations may be offered, however. If about one-third of the land was subject to tenancy and the rents averaged 40% of the gross yield, then the 30-million-ton figure would imply a grain output of 225

million tons. The official estimates of the new regime put the pre-1949 peak output at 138.7 million tons, however, while O. L. Dawson, former U.S. agricultural attaché in China, estimated the pre-1949 peak at 170 million tons (see Table 4-1 below). In the Liao article, however, no distinction is made between the land area subject to redistribution and the portion of that area actually owned by landlords. (As I will show in the text of this chapter, this distinction is an important one.) If Liao treated all the land distributed as land formerly owned by landlords and assumed, as is conventionally done, that one-half of the grain output went for rent, this would imply a grain output of 136 million tons, in line with the official estimate for the pre-1949 peak.

5) The Agrarian Reform Law of the People's Republic of China (Peking, 1950).

6) See Table 4-1 below. The official estimates appear to overstate the rate of recovery, the Dawson estimates to understate it. There is no question, however, but that the recovery was rapid and substantial. Liu and Yeh argue that the rapid recovery presented no problems in light of the primitive technological conditions of Chinese agriculture (p. 53). This view, neglecting the role of managerial and entrepreneurial services as it does (in auxiliary roles of finance, distribution, and transportation as well as in direct production), appears inadequate.

7) Except for land adjacent to major cities, a few large tracts of land for state farms, forest land, and so forth; most of the land remained privately owned.

8) William Hinton, Fanshen (New York, 1966) and C. K. Yang, A Chinese Village in Early Communist Transition (Cambridge, Mass., 1959), reprinted in Chinese Communist Society: The Family and the Village (Cambridge, Mass., 1965).

9) But only 32.2% of the families.

10) The largest private landowner in the village owned 138 mou (23 acres) of land, two draft animals and other cattle, and a small distillery. His other sources of income included moneylending and managing the affairs of a charitable organization and the district Confucian Association (there was no system of

accounts for these organizations, so that he was able to pocket substantial sums). He was also village head for many years, which opened several additional sources of income to him, the most important of which was tax farming. The accumulation of wealth to which these various activities led was enormous in terms of the village standards and could not be measured in terms of land ownership alone. Hinton, pp. 30-32.

11) Following the land reform the support of institutions was, by and large, made the responsibility of the village governments or peasant associations.

12) These and the following data are from Hinton, p. 28.

13) The total of draft animals comes to 99% due to rounding. Poor peasants typically owned no draft animals at all.

14) See Table 3-1.

15) See Table 3-1.

16) See Chapter Two. As noted there, the estimate, based on Buck's survey, may be somewhat on the conservative side, both because of the possible bias in Buck's sample and because the tenancy ratio in 1929-1931, when most of Buck's observations were taken, may have been lower than it became when the full impact of the Great Depression was felt a few years later. If so, the gap between the amount of land tenanted and the amount redistributed would be narrower than that indicated in the text.

17) Liu Shao-chi, "On the Agrarian Reform Law," printed in The Agrarian Reform Law, cited in Note 5 above.

18) These and the following data are from Yang, chs. 2-4.

19) The opportunity cost of making this deposit should properly be included as part of the rent payment. Since funds loaned out could "earn" a very minimum of 20% yearly, we should add 10% to the value of the rent payment (the deposit was equal to half a year's rent), bringing it to a minimum of 52.6% of the net yield.

20) Yang, p. 43.

21) Ibid., p. 155.

22) Ibid., p. 156.

23) Ibid., p. 156.

24) Dwight H. Perkins, Market Control and Planning in Communist China (Cambridge, Mass., 1966), p. 110.

25) The rapid increase in national income and industrial output in the 1950s, moreover, confirms this view. See especially Kang Chao, The Rate and Pattern of Industrial Growth in Communist China (Ann Arbor, 1965), among the many works which provide corroborating data.

26) Nai-Ruenn Chen, ed., Chinese Economic Statistics: A Handbook for Mainland China (Chicago, 1967), p. 441.

27) Ibid., p. 93.

28) Ibid., p. 446.

29) "'Basic construction' refers to the investment which will result in addition to the productive and nonproductive fixed assets" (ibid., p. 20). Investment in "working capital" refers to the increase in [funds used for] "production stocks, semifinished goods, and goods in process (including finished goods not immediately sold). Production stocks consist of raw and basic materials," and so forth (ibid., p. 16).

30) See Table 1 in the Statistical Appendix for net and gross investment figures.

31) Chen, Chinese Economic Statistics, p. 441.

32) There is no way to avoid an arbitrary element in calculating net investment, as it must reflect the somewhat arbitrary assumptions that estimating depreciation always involves. On the other hand, it is net investment, rather than gross, that accounts for the contribution of capital deepening per se to growth (although technological progress can be embodied in gross as well as in net investment). Thus the contribution of the land reform is measured against both the net and gross investment figures.

33) Based on a gross output value of 21.17 billion yuan in 1933. See Chapter One, p. 17.

34) See Table 5 in the Statistical Appendix.

35) Shun-hsin Chou, The Chinese Inflation 1937-1949 (New York, 1963), p. 58.

36) See Chapter One, Note 13.

37) Chen Po-ta, A Study of Land Rent in Pre-Liberation China (Peking, 1966), pp. 70-81.

38) The National Income of Communist China (New York, 1961), p. 154.

39) See Statistical Appendix, Table 2. If valued in 1933 prices, the contribution of the agricultural sector to 1952 national income would be 57% (Liu and Yeh, p. 66). For the reasons described on pp. 107-109 in the text, however, the validity of this comparison is limited.

40) Chang Kia-ngau, The Inflationary Spiral: The Experience in China, 1939-1950 (New York, 1958), pp. 9-12.

41) Perkins, p. 111.

42) For all manufacturing in the U.S. from 1949 to 1958 the after-tax rate, excluding the distributors' profits on sales, was 3.9%, or about 8% before corporate income taxes; for leading firms the latter figure was more commonly in the 10-15% range (which corresponded to approximately a 20-25% rate of return on equity). For light industry, with a lower capital intensity and higher level of sales per dollar of capital stock, the rate of return on sales tended to be lower. Claude Robinson, Understanding Profits (Princeton, 1961), pp. 410, 446-53.

43) See Statistical Appendix, part B of Table 8. As argued in the text, such data can support the conclusions reached there but cannot in themselves be regarded as definitive.

44) See the discussion in Audrey Donnithorne, China's Economic System (London, 1967), p. 346.

45) Ibid., pp. 345-47.

46) Ibid., p. 358. Donnithorne cites A. Nove, The Soviet Economy, p. 105, to the effect that almost 90% of the wholesale price of wheat was accounted for by tax in 1936 in the Soviet Union.

47) Donnithorne, pp. 358-59.

48) Renmin Ribao [People's Daily], October 25, 1959, p. 6.

49) Donnithorne, pp. 360-61.

50) Ibid., p. 362.

51) Ibid., p. 356.

52) It may have contributed indirectly, as low food prices for urban workers could have been used to hold down money wages and thereby increase the profits and/or tax payments of industrial firms. This contribution will already have been reflected in the "excess" profits, described in the text above, which the state gained from industrial sales to the agricultural sector.

53) Perkins, p. 28.

54) See Table 4-1 for agricultural output estimates.

55) Franz Schurmann argues that this was true even through collectivization (in 1955-1956), until the formation of the communes (in 1958). Ideology and Organization in Communist China (Berkeley, 1966), p. 470.

56) See Shigeru Ishikawa, Economic Development in Asian Perspective (Tokyo, 1967), p. 77.

57) See the Statistical Appendix, Table 9.

58) Land reform generally can be expected to makes its contribution to production only over an extended period of time. See the discussion in Chapters One and Four.

59) As explained in the text above, the increase in the capacity of the agricultural sector to bear increased exactions is indissolubly linked to the land reform. To assign responsibility to the land reform is not, however, meant to deny the complementary role played by other factors. The 5.04 billion yuan figure excludes the 1.6 billion yuan estimated self-investment in agriculture noted in the section on self-investment above for the reasons discussed there.

60) See Statistical Appendix, Table 2.

61) See Statistical Appendix, Table 2.

62) All of these proportions are derived from the data presented in Chapter Two.

63) See the Statistical Appendix, Table 2, for the value data on which this calculation is based.

64) See the Statistical Appendix, Table 2.

65) There is no absolute criterion for associating a given

item of income with a given use of income when there are several sources and several uses. Proper treatment of this issue depends, then, on the reasonableness of the assumptions. Tax revenue is an ordinary source of revenue for all governments and commonly serves to finance both public consumption and public investment. The income from control over relative prices is, by contrast, extraordinary and can most reasonably be regarded as contributing to expenditures that range beyond the ordinary administrative functions of government — in this case public investment.

CHAPTER FOUR

The land reform in international
and historical context

The land reform brought a complete transformation of the economic structure of rural China. Its ramifications were so widespread and inevitably affected so many variables in the economic process that oversimplified assertions concerning its impact should be treated with caution. Even so, the connecting lines between the land reform and certain key variables are sufficiently distinct to permit analysis and es'.imation, while the issues involved are of sufficient importance to lend validity to the effort. An increase in the national savings-investment ratio typically plays a central role in any development program, and it is the interconnection between this ratio and the land reform that has served as the focus of the analytic efforts of this study. One more or less self-contained structure of income and expenditure existed in the rural sector of traditional China and was replaced by a new one as a consequence of the land reform. Given the diversion of income streams and transformation of the economic environment brought about by the land reform, there is no reason other than coincidence to expect the level of savings generated by the two structures to be identical. In fact, there are compelling reasons for believing that the economic organization of traditional China hindered saving and that, although characterized by conflicting forces, the new structure was, on balance, conducive to an increase in saving.

The land reform played a central role in transforming the

traditional structure and in making possible the use of a substantial share of the agricultural surplus to finance investment.
The alternative of taxing the agricultural sector severely while
leaving the existing production relations intact is unlikely to
have produced the same results. Such a policy would have invited reduced production and marketing efforts, a disincentive
consequence which the new regime could not afford: the margin
between food-grain production and subsistence requirements
was too narrow. Further, this type of policy would not have
confronted the problem of nonproductive employment (and use
of resources) generated by the traditional landholding system
itself. Moreover, the substantial costs of administration and
collection, magnified by the inevitable resistance, would have
curtailed net receipts. While this type of argument is necessarily conjectural, since we can only speculate as to what might
have happened if alternative policies had been followed, it appears that any attempt to manipulate the terms of trade against
agriculture while leaving the traditional institutional structure
intact would have encountered the same difficulties.

The rationale of the land reform in terms of political economy stretches, of course, far beyond these points. The revolution was undertaken to benefit the peasants, to eliminate social
inequity, and to lay the basis for the creation of an advanced
socialist economy and society. These objectives could not be
accomplished as long as the landlord maintained a claim, however tenuous, on rural product. It is evident that confiscatory
taxation could have been used, but that is just confiscation under
another name. Besides being less suited to the achievement of
the multiple objectives noted above, such a course of action
would have been less desirable in terms of China's development
strategy, as it would have required returning investment funds
to peasants through government intermediaries, reducing the
directness of their participation in the saving and investment
process. It would also have hindered the development of collective agriculture. The subsequent collectivization, in turn,
was essential to the utilization of China's major underemployed

resource, labor, which could not have been mobilized on the scale it was if family-sized farms remained. The land reform, then, by changing the institutional structure in China's country-side, at once solidified support for the new regime, increased the income of those who needed it most, laid the basis for egal-itarian, socialist economic development, and channeled a portion of the agricultural surplus into increased national savings and investment. While these multiple objectives could not have been achieved simultaneously without the land reform, the focus of this investigation has been on the contribution of the land re-form to raising the national savings-investment ratio.

The principal theoretical considerations bearing on this pro-cess were elaborated in Chapter One and need not be repeated here. Chapter Two provided, in essence, a picture of the cir-cular flow of income and expenditure in the rural economy of traditional China, focusing in particular on some of the major constituents of the property share of income. Chapter Three investigated the new structure, the saving which it generated, the manner in which the saving was mobilized, and the role played by the land reform in the emergence of the new pat-terns. At this point a brief review of the findings of Chap-ters Two and Three in the light of the algebraic and class models of Chapter One may help to bind together the whole discussion.

Equation (3) from page 16, Chapter One, is repeated below:

$$Y_t = rQ + r'Q + iL_{tp} = C_t + S_t + M_t \qquad (3)$$

This listing of the income sources of rural property owners in traditional China is not complete; commercial profits in par-ticular were undoubtedly substantial, but the data deficiencies here are so severe as to preclude reasonable estimation. Thus Y_t, while it encompasses most of the principal property share income components in rural China, does not include all of them. The calculations of Chapter Two have shown that rQ (rental in-come) in 1933 was 3,099 million yuan; $r'Q$ (the surplus produced by hired labor) 982 million yuan; and iL_{tp} (interest income) 821 million yuan, so that Y_t in that year was 4,902 million yuan, which in turn represented close to 17% of China's net domestic product in 1933. With S_t limited and its role in financing productive investment close to zero, the opportunity cost — the financing of productive investment sacrificed — of redirecting these property income flows to poor and landless peasants was likewise close to zero.

The redistribution of property and income itself is expressed in equation (7), which is also repeated here:

$$\Delta Y_p = rQ + r'Q + iL_{tp} = \Delta C_p + \Delta S_p + \Delta M_p \qquad (7)$$

The equation traces the disposition of the share of national income which the poor and landless peasants gained through the land reform. This share was smaller in 1952, when it amounted to 13.1% of net domestic product, than in 1933, due to the diminished share of agriculture in national income in 1952 as compared with the earlier year. (1) As indicated in the conclusion to Chapter Three, the initial gain from redistribution ($rQ + r'Q + iL_{tp}$) may have amounted to 9.39 billion yuan (in 1952 prices) out of a net domestic product in that year of 71.41 billion yuan. Of the gain, 5.48 billion yuan constituted ΔM_p and 3.91 billion yuan ΔC_p plus ΔS_p, where ΔC_p plus ΔS_p represents the gain in peasant disposable income. The 3.91 billion yuan figure understates the real gain in peasant disposable income as it does not include the peasant gains from the abolition of illegal and semilegal charges which the land reform brought about.

ΔM_p shows the portion of the peasant gains from the land reform which the government extracted for public purposes. It is composed of two elements: gains from maintaining urban-rural terms of trade adverse to agriculture (3.88 billion yuan) and gains from increased taxation (1.60 billion yuan). In evaluating the contribution of the land reform to national savings, however, the entire post-land-reform agricultural tax, 2.70 billion

yuan, has been treated as constituting a fund for potential investment, a fund which was used for this purpose in the same
proportion, 43%, that investment constituted of public expenditures. Thus agricultural taxation can be regarded as responsible for 1.16 billion yuan of national saving and gains from the
manipulation of the terms of trade 3.88 billion yuan; and the
total contribution of the land reform to national savings can be
set at 5.04 billion yuan, representing 44.8% and 34.7% of 1952's
net and gross investment, respectively.

While the land reform was not responsible for the majority
of development finance in 1952, its contribution was both substantial and compatible with an increase in living standards for
its poor and landless peasant beneficiaries. Consideration of
these results in the light of the scheme of class divisions presented in Chapter One* can further illuminate the conclusions.

Almost all of the 9.39 billion yuan redistributed reflects a
drop in the consumption of class 1. This figure does not, however, encompass that consumption supported by commercial
and speculator profits in the rural sector. Furthermore, the
diminished employment and income in class 2 has not entered
into the direct calculations. It has been shown in Chapter Two,
however, that a pervasive network of economic relations and
gainful activities existed as part of the infrastructure of land-
owner-dominated rural China, the elimination of which also
reduced membership and consumption in classes 1 and 2, thereby increasing the possibilities for expanded employment and
output in classes 3 and 4. The understatement these omissions
involve does not affect the calculations upon which the estimate
of 5.04 billion (1952) yuan going to finance expanded output and
employment in class 4 was based; the omissions, rather, understate the increase in output, employment, and consumption in
class 3. Thus the exclusion of the auxiliary network of economic relations from the calculations does not affect the estimate of land reform's contribution to the national savings-

---

*See p. 21.

investment ratio but leads to an understatement of the increase in popular consumption (in employment and output in class 3, the producers of subsistence goods and services) which accompanied it.

China's land reform, then, played a major role in raising the national savings-investment ratio and thereby accelerating the development and modernization of China's economy after 1950. The redistribution of income which it entailed made the increase in savings and investment compatible with an increase in consumption on the part of the greater portion of the Chinese people.

The Chinese experience in the light of world experience with land reform

The impact of land reform on savings and investment can be considered either through its effect on income distribution or through its effect on agricultural productivity. As the discussion of Chapters One and Three indicated, the influence of China's land reform on the national savings rate was felt principally through its effect on income distribution. The redirection of income flows was not in itself a condition sufficient to raise savings, however; a national administration committed to development and willing and able to extract a portion of the gains from land reform's immediate beneficiaries for this purpose also played an indispensable role. Since it was the combination of these two elements that was responsible for raising the savings ratio in China's case, the presence or absence of a like combination deserves primary attention in making comparisons with the land reform experience of other countries.

When the question is put in these terms, the uniqueness of China's experience becomes evident immediately. While land reform implies "the redistribution of property or rights in land for the benefit of small farmers and agricultural laborers" (2), so that the element of income redistribution is a corollary of land reform, what has existed in no country other than China is the role played by the public sector. To tax away most of the gains of land reform, while nominally possible, has not been carried through systematically anywhere (China included); such an effort would involve directly contravening the very political forces which give rise to land reform in the first place. Control over the terms of trade between industry and agriculture must supplement income redistribution and increased taxes, therefore, in using land reform to increase national savings. Such control, to be effective in increasing saving, typically requires public control over wholesale trade and public ownership of the means of production in the industrial sector. These conditions, in turn, are present in relatively few of the countries which have carried out a genuine land reform. (3) Thus while the nature of land reform is very much shaped by local conditions, so that no two reforms can be precisely alike, the singularity of the Chinese experience is particularly marked. Elsewhere, the influence of land reform on savings and investment has come about chiefly through its impact on agricultural productivity.

Historically, the principal thrust behind land reform has been political and social, with the redistribution of property rights perceived as a means of securing the more equitable distribution of agricultural product. The economic arguments which envision land reform as a means of stimulating growth are of more recent vintage. They start with the observation that underdeveloped countries as a group organize their agricultural activity in a way which differs markedly from the progressive and progressing agricultural activity in the advanced countries, where, for example, latifundia or Asian-style landowner-tenant relations are not to be found. The inferences drawn from this are that the organizational structure of agriculture in underdeveloped countries acts as an impediment in the way of increasing output and that some form of land reform, by removing the institutional obstacles to development, will pave the way to an increased output of farm products. The first of these inferences is justified; the second is more problematical.

The actual world experience with land reform has led to mixed results. It seems clear that where followed by heavy public investment (Italy) or a substantial improvement in auxiliary public services or inputs (improved seeds and so forth, as in Egypt), land reform can contribute to improved performance in the agricultural sector. (4) In Mexico the rapid long-term growth of agricultural output which followed land reform must be credited to the larger properties which remained after the distribution of the marginal properties of the latifundia; whether this is due to more efficient farm size or a shift in owner motivation (to a concern with more efficient practices when the size of his holding is reduced) cannot, however, be readily ascertained. While direct assistance with complementary production requirements was not significant here, once again the impact of the land reform cannot be understood in isolation; the link between agriculture's performance and the expansion of markets associated with the industrialization of the Mexican economy must be considered.

These are essentially longer-run experiences. In the short run, any adverse effects will be compounded by the problems of transition. In Bolivia (1953) and Iraq (1958) declines in agricultural output over the three years following land reform may have reached 50% or more. (5) While these examples are striking, any attempt to draw a simplistic dichotomy between beneficial long-range effects and negative short-range ones should be rejected. (6) Moreover, the size of production units in agriculture does not in itself determine the growth capacity of the sector, since the success of agricultural development in some countries where large farms predominate has matched that of some where typical units are much smaller. No unqualified assertions can be made, therefore, about the impact of land reform on agricultural output — too much depends on the nature of the land reform in question and the extent to which production needs which complement the organizational ones are taken care of. Empirical evidence attests to the fact that a well thought

out land reform program can, where complementary needs are
satisfied, contribute over time to raising agricultural productivity. But it is precisely this longer-range potentiality which
can never be evaluated in the Chinese case because further
institutional change followed in a few years. This further
change — collectivization — has been the subject of many studies in its own right. Here it will be considered from a limited
perspective: the light it casts upon the land reform it succeeded.

The land reform
and agricultural collectivization

As the discussion of Chapter One indicated, China's land reform was more than a ruse to gain popular support. While collectivization was always a longer-range goal, it was felt when
the socialist regime came to power that collectivization was an
organizational form whose rationale depended upon substantial
material support from the industrial sector of the economy,
support which could only be forthcoming after a prolonged
period of sustained development. While large-scale organization was believed superior, its advantages appeared capable of
realization only when accompanied by a substantial increase in
capital inputs. In the early 1950s, then, the agrarian structure
left by land reform was expected to endure for some time,
modified principally by the gradual increase in mutual aid
teams (7), part of a program of step-by-step progress toward
the distant goal of collectivization. (8) By the end of 1955, however, only three years after land reform had been mainly completed, most of the farm population had entered producer cooperatives, which became "advanced stage cooperatives" or full
collectives only a year later, when the return to the land and
capital contributed was eliminated. The unexpected haste with
which collectivization was carried out and the reasons behind
it cast considerable light on the nature and limitations of the
land reform's contribution to development.

The land reform brought with it a rapid recovery of production

to the peak levels which had been reached in the prewar period.
This was achieved despite the disrupting influences which will
accompany any such reform program (9), primarily because
the traditional pattern of farming was not fundamentally dis-
turbed. The landlord was primarily a rentier: having made no
contribution to production before the reform, his subsequent
disappearance made no impact either. But while the preservation of the traditional organization of farming facilitated the
recovery in agricultural output, it also set distinct limits on
the expansion of that output. Small, fragmented, undercapital-
ized farms dominated the countryside, and there was no path
to facilitate the introduction of new practices and technology.
The performance of Chinese agriculture under these conditions,
as well as under the subsequent cooperativization, collectivization, and communization, is reflected in Table 4-1.

    While estimates of China's grain output in the last two decades
can only hope to indicate approximate orders of magnitude, it
is evident that progress was made in the 1952-1955 period but
that that progress was modest. During this time, some of the
gains were absorbed by population increase, some by larger
per capita consumption, as government procurement difficulties
and the "planned purchase and planned supply" and "three fix"
policies confirm. Moreover, over this period the terms of
trade with the industrial sector were shifting slowly back in
favor of the rural population from the adverse terms which
existed at the beginning of the period. (10) This situation was
reflected in a steady increase in the supply of industrial goods
to rural villages (11), while the flow of agricultural products
in the opposite direction increased much more modestly. The
agricultural sector, lagging far behind the industrial sector in
productivity growth, became a bottleneck constraining further
growth on a national level. Thus the contribution to development
finance which land reform entailed could not be sustained without more substantial productivity growth in the agricultural
sector.

    Under these circumstances, the planned transition from the

organization of agriculture with which the land reform had left China to a succession of collectivized forms was accelerated (12), the basic unit of accounting and distribution ultimately settling down to a team of about 20-40 families in the 1960s, following a period of experimentation with larger-sized units. From 1954 the argument that full-scale collectivization had to await China's capacity to mechanize agriculture was set aside. (13) Rather, it was argued that the reorganization of production activities in agriculture could in itself raise productivity and was, in fact, a precondition for effective mechanization. The collectives were justified economically largely in terms of the more rational allocation of labor and more intensive use of labor which it was believed they would make possible. In his studies of Chinese agriculture in the early 1930s, Buck found that able-bodied men were, on the average, idle 1.7 months per year. (14) Most of this was seasonal unemployment concentrated in the winter months. Collectivization, it was argued, would make possible fuller use of this underemployed labor in social overhead capital formation, especially in irrigation and other water-conservancy projects, as well as more intensive use of labor during the growing season. Agricultural productivity would also be enhanced, it was argued, by the consolidation of scattered strips, elimination of the boundaries between them, and unified land-use planning. An additional advantage in this latter change was also seen in its bringing agricultural activity within the scope of national economic planning to a greater degree. Finally, the arguments that collectivization would make possible more timely production activities and the more efficient use of complementary inputs than would be possible when those inputs were separately owned by different individuals, arguments which had been put forth on behalf of the mutual aid teams, reappeared on an expanded scale.

The problems of analysis and interpretation which collectivization raises are legion; they will not be dealt with here. The purpose of this brief overview has been to set the land reform in its historical context.

Table 4-1

Organizational Forms, Output, and Productivity in Chinese Agriculture

Year	Crop weather	Organizational forms (through 1957, % farm households)	Grain output (millions of tons)		Yield† (metric tons per hectare)		
			Official estimates	Dawson's estimates*	Rice	Wheat	Other grains
pre-1949 peak			138.7	170			
1949	poor		108.1	150			
1951		team‡ 19.2% autumn	154.4	170			
1952	good	team 39.9% autumn	156.9	166	2.62	0.8	1.0
1953	average	team 39.3% autumn	160.5	170			
1954	poor	team 58.4% autumn; coop‡ 4.7% autumn					
1955	good	coop 14.2% spring; coop 59.3% Dec.; coll.‡ 4.0% Dec.	174.8	185			
1956	poor	coll. 54.9% March; coll. 63.2% June; coop 28.7% June	182.5	175–80			
1957	average	coop 3.7% June; coll. 93.3% June	185.0	185	2.60	0.86	1.04
1958//	good	[Colls. dominant to August. Then people's communes to present. Within the communes, the basic unit of accounting and distribution was de-	250.0	204			
1959//	average		270.0	170			
1960§	poor		150.0	160			
1961	poor		162.0	170	2.50	0.70	0.87

1962	good	centralized from the commune level to the production brigades (about 100–350 households) in the spring of 1959 and to the production teams (about 20–40 households) from 1961.]	174.0	180
1963	average		183.0	185
1964	good		200.0	195
1965	average		200.0	193–200	2.96	0.85
1970#			240.0				1.00

Sources:

1. Edwin F. Jones, "The Emerging Pattern of China's Economic Revolution," An Economic Profile of Mainland China, pp. 93–94.

2. Kenneth R. Walker, Planning in Chinese Agriculture, pp. 16–17.

3. Kenneth R. Walker, "Collectivisation in Retrospect," The China Quarterly, April-June 1966, pp. 13, 16–18, 34–35.

4. Franz Schurmann, Ideology and Organization in Communist China, p. 454.

5. New York Times, March 13, 1971.

Notes:

*O. L. Dawson was formerly the U.S. agricultural attaché in China.

†The yield estimates were carefully compiled by Edwin Jones according to the procedure he describes in the work cited above, p. 94. They are the best available, although, as is the case with the output estimates, a good deal of conjecture is unavoidable.

‡"Team" refers to the mutual aid teams of 7–8 households. "Coop" refers to the primary stage agricultural producer cooperatives; and "coll." (collective) to the advanced stage ones.

§Since 1960, official data have not been published, but Chinese officials have discussed food output levels with foreigners.

‖The official data for 1958–1959 are guesses made during the breakdown of the statistical system: they wildly overstate actual output and should not be considered seriously.

#The 1970 figure is that given to journalist Edgar Snow by Premier Chou En-lai. Cited in the New York Times, March 13, 1971. It compares with a planned target (cited by Jones) of 243.0 million tons and suggests that the performance of agriculture in the second half of the 1960s approximately met official targets.

The land reform made a major contribution to raising the national level of saving and investment in China in the early 1950s. It did so through redirecting the pattern of prevailing income flows at a turning point in history, allowing both an increase in consumption on the part of the poorest peasants and an increase in savings in the agricultural sector. Without purposeful public policy, a much larger share of the gains of redistribution would have taken the form of increased consumption. But while the land reform was capable of promoting a sharp spurt in the share of national income devoted to savings and investment, it was incapable of leading to immediate breakthroughs in agricultural productivity. Although its immediate contribution to development, then, was limited to its redistributional effect, this contribution was distinct and essential. The higher levels of saving and investment which China's land reform helped create made possible the substantial increase in output and diversification which the Chinese economy displayed in the 1950s, besides providing the margin within which the continued experimentation with new institutional forms to facilitate China's socialist economic development could take place.

Notes

1) Net domestic product in 1952 was 71.41 billion yuan, and net value added in agriculture in the same year was 34.19 billion yuan, both in 1952 prices. See Statistical Appendix, Table 2.

2) Doreen Warriner, Land Reform in Principle and Practice (Oxford, 1969), p. xiv.

3) While these conditions were present in the Soviet Union and Eastern Europe, no land reform in the sense of property redistribution for the benefit of small peasants and agricultural laborers took place there. Rather, the institutional reorganization of the agricultural sector was designed primarily to extract resources to finance industrialization, marking a strong

contrast to the situation in China, where dual objectives existed and were met.

4) See the excellent discussion of these and the following
cases in Warriner.

5) Philip Raup, "Land Reform and Agricultural Development," in Agricultural Development and Economic Growth, ed.
H. M. Southworth and B. F. Johnston (Ithaca, 1967), p. 289.

6) Warriner discusses Cuba as one instance where, within
a limited time horizon, the experience was reversed.

7) About eight families, living and owning land and farm
equipment separately, but pooling their labor for farm work.

8) Kenneth Walker provides a comprehensive discussion
of this policy in "Collectivisation in Retrospect," The China
Quarterly, April-June 1966. Among the numerous references
he cites (p. 3) are Liao Kai-lung ("only by first carrying out
industrialisation can we refit Chinese agriculture with agricultural machinery, and only then on a basis of the peasants'
agreement, can we carry out full collectivisation") and Teng
Tzu-hui ("[we must] wait until State industrial development is
able to supply agriculture with the machinery it needs, and at
that time Soviet type collective farms, using machines, can
gradually grow in China and greatly spread"). Both were writing in Chinese journals in 1953.

9) Such as, in the Chinese case, inadequacies in livestock
maintenance and agricultural credit.

10) See the discussion in Chapter Three and Table 8 in the
Statistical Appendix.

11) See Table 3-3.

12) Other factors, including especially the tendency of class
polarization to reappear, also played an important part in the
decision to speed collectivization.

13) See the excellent discussion of this situation in Walker,
op. cit.

14) Buck, Land Utilization in China, p. 294.

Statistical appendix

The classic study of Chinese agricultural conditions, in which 16,786 farms in twenty-two provinces were surveyed between 1929 and 1933, was carried out under the direction of John Lossing Buck; the results appear in his three-volume Land Utilization in China. The observations cited are quite reliable — they were obtained under the direction of trained investigators and assembled by professional statisticians. Possible biases have been noted in the text: wealthier households and north and east China may have received undue representation; institutional land was not included in the tenancy data; and much of the data was collected prior to the full impact of the Great Depression on the Chinese economy.

Buck's work in particular served to introduce Western empirical methods in social science research and met with an enthusiastic response from Chinese intellectuals, many of whom were stimulated to carry out field investigations of their own, although of course on a more localized basis. The Western origin of their stimulus and continued interest in their work explains the ready availability in English of the principal studies. These scholars typically sought to publish their works in Chinese and English simultaneously, and subsequent translation was often possible (e.g., Agrarian China) even where publication was originally in Chinese. The extent of the desire to communicate with the English-speaking world can hardly be overstated; even Chinese government agencies published

English versions of their principal research efforts, as in the case of the encyclopedic provincial studies (e.g., Kiangsu, Chekiang, Honan) of economic conditions that were completed before the outbreak of World War II terminated such efforts.

There is really no way to assess directly the reliability of many of these empirical studies, although there is no reason whatsoever to doubt the sincerity of the investigators. The existence of a large number of such studies carried out independently is most helpful, however, as it makes possible crosschecking their results. Other information also helps in interpretation: the greater productivity of land in the south, for example, accords with the higher rentals generally observed there. Finally, some of the observers, such as Fei Hsiao-tung, were particularly capable and precise; their work helps in assessing the reasonableness of other reports. When all is said and done, however, some range of ambiguity does exist, and it is for this reason that the effects of alternative assumptions are explored in the Appendix to Chapter Two.

The principal Chinese language sources are Materials on China's Modern Agricultural History, Vol. 3, 1927-1937 and Selected Statistical Materials on China's Modern Economic History. Both volumes emerged as part of the new regime's larger effort in the 1950s to systematically collect data on China's economic history. The two works cited, like the others which this effort produced, consist of compilations of data gathered from a wide variety of sources, but especially journal reports and (Kuomintang) government studies, interspersed with editorial introductions interpreting the data from a Marxian standpoint. The data themselves are not revised but presented as they originally appeared. The value of the collections lies in their making available in compact form data from a wide variety of frequently obscure sources; the value of the underlying data is determined by the quality of the original sources. There is no effort made in the collections to interpret the quality of the data. While the accuracy of these data cannot ordinarily be directly ascertained, as is the case with the materials cited above, they serve as one more source for cross-checking other data and can themselves be cross-checked in the same fashion.

While the Chinese government has suppressed the publication and dissemination of economic data since 1960, both for propaganda and security purposes, a wealth of information concerning the 1950s has been made public; the availability of data on the Chinese economy during the 1950s compares quite favorably with that for most underdeveloped countries. In the United States especially, much effort has gone into systematically compiling and analyzing these data, if not into creative interpretation. The comprehensive national income accounts worked out by Liu and Yeh, The Economy of the Chinese Mainland, are among the foremost achievements in this regard. Since, moreover, their studies cover precisely the period in which I am interested, I have used their results liberally. At some points, however, the inevitable gaps in the data have led them to use estimating procedures subject to a wide margin of error; I have noted such cases, where relevant, in the text. Readers interested in the methodology they use should consult the work directly.

Table 1

Domestic Expenditure by End Use, 1933 and 1952-1957

	1933 (billions of 1933 yuan)	1933	1952	1953	1954	1955	1956	1957
				(billions of 1952 yuan)				
1. Personal consumption	28.02	56.53	54.60	51.84	54.96	56.99	62.60	64.69
a. Food	18.13	33.19	33.08	33.59	36.44	36.35	36.64	38.39
b. Clothing	2.17	7.56	7.89	8.79	8.43	7.82	10.40	9.62
c. Fuel and light	2.16	4.49	5.11	5.22	5.35	5.46	5.58	5.72
d. Housing	1.37	2.66	3.04	3.10	3.16	3.25	3.31	3.40
e. Miscellaneous	4.19	8.63	5.48	1.14	1.58	4.11	6.67	7.36
2. Communal services	0.14	0.32	1.94	2.45	2.46	2.32	3.26	3.29
3. Government consumption	1.06	2.36	5.34	6.64	5.49	6.11	5.23	5.92
4. Net domestic investment	0.51	2.55	11.26	15.45	16.74	18.04	20.39	20.62
5. Net domestic expenditure	29.73	61.76	73.14	76.38	79.65	83.46	91.48	94.32
6. Depreciation	1.02	2.19	3.26	3.66	4.03	4.27	5.20	5.48
7. Gross domestic expenditure	30.75	63.95	76.40	80.04	83.68	87.73	96.68	99.80
8. Net domestic investment as % of net domestic expenditure (line 4 as % of line 5)	1.72	4.13	15.40	20.23	21.02	21.62	22.29	21.86

Source: Liu and Yeh, The Economy of the Chinese Mainland, p. 68.

Table 2

Domestic Product by Industrial Origin

Net value added in:	1933 (billions of 1933 yuan)	1952	1933 (billions of 1952 yuan)	1952	% of net dom. product (1933 in 1933 prices)
1. Agriculture	18.76	18.39	33.86	34.19	65.0
2. Factories	0.64	1.09	3.33	6.45	2.2
a. Producers' goods	0.16	0.46	0.84	3.15	
b. Consumers' goods	0.47	0.63	2.48	3.30	
3. Handicrafts	2.04	2.14	4.41	4.72	7.1
4. Mining	0.21	0.63	0.50	1.47	0.7
5. Utilities	0.13	0.31	0.14	0.31	0.5
6. Construction	0.34	0.60	1.03	1.83	1.2
7. Modern transpor-tation and com-munications	0.43	0.83	1.09	2.10	1.5
8. Old-fashioned transportation	1.20	1.20	2.61	2.65	4.2
9. Trade	2.71	2.88	8.19	9.66	9.4
a. Traditional stores and restaurants	1.75	1.97	6.12	7.66	
b. Peddlers	0.96	0.91	2.07	2.00	
10. Government administration	0.82	1.84	1.43	3.27	2.8
11. Finance	0.21	0.80	0.35	1.31	0.7
12. Personal services	0.34	0.34	0.55	0.55	1.2
13. Residential rents	1.03	1.17	2.00	2.28	3.6
14. Work brigades		0.28		0.62	
Net Domestic Product	28.86	32.50	59.49	71.41	
Depreciation	1.02	1.33	2.19	3.26	
Gross Domestic Product	29.88	33.83	61.68	74.67	

Source: Liu and Yeh, The Economy of the Chinese Mainland, p. 66.

Table 3

National Government Cash Receipts and Payments for Years Ending Dates Shown
(in Chinese dollars)

Receipts

		June 30, 1933		June 30, 1934
Revenue:				
Customs		$325,534,850		$352,398,559
Salt		158,073,565		177,375,273
Consolidated taxes:		79,596,999		104,977,964
a. Rolled tobacco	$53,680,781		$70,910,039	
b. Flour	5,529,135		5,784,548	
c. Cotton yarn	15,415,838		17,986,916	
d. Match	4,069,275		4,884,564	
e. Cement	901,967		1,853,823	
f. Cured tobacco			3,558,072	
Tobacco and wine		9,506,988		13,073,584
Stamp tax		5,118,580		8,378,911
Government railways		20,249,995		16,781,162
Miscellaneous		15,760,350		16,502,875
Total revenue		613,841,331*		689,488,337†
Less: support of revenue services		54,512,246		67,048,909
refunds		21,869		780,470
Net total		559,307,213		621,658,957
Net proceeds from borrowing:		112,617,542		179,959,332
Total receipts		$671,924,755		$801,618,289

Table 3 (continued)

Payments

	June 30, 1933	June 30, 1934
Party	$ 4,756,172	$ 5,589,584
Net payments for civil purposes	77,970,957	98,893,495
of which subsidies to provincial and local governments:	$29,230,321	$26,038,121
Military expenses	320,672,116†	372,895,202§
Loan service (net)	169,541,348	202,601,983
Local authorities from salt revenue	37,254,869	23,003,728
Special fund accounting from salt revenue	574,459	942,222
Indemnity (net)	40,507,533	41,676,254
Net increase in reserve and suspense items	(−6,446,100)	23,519,882
Increase in cash balances	27,093,398‖	32,495,934
Total payments	$671,924,755	$801,618,289

Source: The China Year Book 1936, pp. 385-86.

Notes:

*Evidently due to rounding, the totals listed sometimes differ by a few dollars from the sum of the constituent items listed.

†While the figure shown in the source ends in the three digits 377, this appears to be an error

Table 3 (continued)

as it is not consistent with the other figures shown. It has been corrected to the most probable figure.

‡Including payments made in prior years of Chin. $58,805,349. This notation, which may result from a confusion in accounting concepts, is taken directly from the source, although its presence in a cash budget is inexplicable.

§Including payments made in prior years of Chin. $46,376,864.

‖While this figure is listed as the cash balance at the end of the year, there is no figure in the fiscal 1933 budget for cash balance at the beginning of the year. Since the receipts and payments balance only if this figure is treated as the increase in cash balances, I have treated it in this manner here.

Table 4

The Proportion of Military Expenditure and Loan and
Indemnity Service in National Government Payments
(unit: Chinese dollars)

Year ending June 30	Military expenditure*		Loan and indemnity service	
	Amount	% of net total payments	Amount	% of net total payments
1929	$210,000,000	50.8	$158,000,000	38.3
1930	245,000,000	45.5	200,000,000	37.2
1931	312,000,000	43.6	290,000,000	40.5
1932	304,000,000	44.5	270,000,000	39.5
1933	321,000,000	49.7	210,000,000	32.6
1934	373,000,000	48.5	244,000,000	31.8

Source: The China Year Book 1935, p. 494.

Note:

*The military expenditure data are said to include payments
made in prior years amounting to $46,000,000 in 1933-1934,
$59,000,000 in 1932-1933, and $49,000,000 in 1931-1932. This
rather strange notation is not explained in the source.

Table 5

Total* Provincial Budget Income
and Expenditures, 1933-1934[†]
(unit: Chinese dollars)

Income	
Land tax	$ 88,385,026
Business taxes	49,021,578
Net profit from government enterprises and properties	6,110,270
Administrative receipts	10,430,884
Subsidies	23,880,695
Other income	102,872,951
Total income	$280,701,404
Expenditures	
General administration	$ 45,007,412
Public safety	45,159,446
Education	39,500,024
Other expenditures [‡]	174,019,067
Total expenditures[§]	$303,685,949

Notes:

* The data are the totals for the individual provincial budgets
listed in The China Year Book 1936, pp. 389-93. Not all prov-
inces were listed. Those represented include Anhwei, Chahar,
Chekiang, Chinghai, Fukien, Honan, Hopei, Hunan, Hupeh,
Kansu, Kiangsi, Kiangsu, Kwangsi, Kwangtung, Kweichow,
Ninghsia, Shansi, Shantung, Shensi, Sinkiang, and Yunnan.

[†]The data for Kwangtung and Shensi are for 1931-1932, those
for Kwangsi 1932-1933, and those for Kansu 1934-1935.

[‡]Other expenditures include Party, financial administration,
judicial, industry, public health, reconstruction, debt service, etc.

[§]In the context of a rather large number of ambiguous accounting
practices, some of the state budgets do not show a balance between
income and expenditure. This accounts for the difference between
total income and total expenditures that appears above.

Table 6

Rural Interest Rates in China, 1933-1934

Province	Cash Credit		Foodgrain Credit	
	Farmers in debt (%)	Annual interest (%)	Farmers in debt (%)	Monthly interest (%)
Chahar	79	32	53	8.3
Suiyuan	48	32	33	7.7
Ningsia	51	37	47	11.7
Tsinghai	56	27	46	5.1
Kansu	63	53	53	7.3
Shensi	66	51	56	14.9
Shansi	61	46	40	6.0
Hopeh	51	29	33	3.3
Shantung	46	34	36	3.5
Honan	41	35	43	7.3
Kiangsu	62	35	50	7.6
Anhwei	63	41	56	10.0
Chekiang	67	20	48	4.0
Fukien	55	21	49	4.7
Kwangtung	60	27	52	5.8
Kiangsi	57	25	52	4.4
Hupeh	46	29	51	6.9
Hunan	52	33	49	6.8
Kwangsi	51	34	58	10.9
Szechwan	56	38	46	5.7
Yunnan	46	35	49	7.2
Kweichow	45	36	47	7.4
Average	56	34	48	7.1

Source: Silver and Prices in China. (Report of the committee
established by the Ministry of Industries for the study of silver
values and commodity prices.) Shanghai, 1935.

Notes:

The original source is Crop Reports (in Chinese), Vol. 2
(April 1934), a publication of the National Agricultural Research

Table 6 (continued)

Bureau. The information was obtained in December 1933, and covered 850 hsien (counties) in twenty-two provinces.

Silver and Prices in China also indicates the percentage of borrowers receiving credit from different sources. Citing the same original source, Materials on China's Modern Agricultural History, Vol. 3 (in Chinese), p. 357, breaks down the percentage of cash loans falling in different interest ranges for each province.

The grain loans were typically of short-term duration.

Table 7

The Ratio of Marketed Portion to Total
Production of Food Grains

Year	Ratio (%)
1952	23.3
1953	24.9
1954	30.8
1955	26.8
1956	21.4
1957	27.2
1958	23.0
1959	24.3

Source: Shigeru Ishikawa, Economic Development in Asian Perspective, p. 312.

Table 8

Terms of Trade Between Chinese Agriculture and Industry:
Indices of Prices Received and Paid by Farmers

A. 1926-1933 (1926 = 100)

Year	Prices received by farmers	Prices paid by farmers
1926	100	100
1927	95	103
1928	106	109
1929	127	118
1930	125	126
1931	116	135
1932	103	127
1933	71	104

Source: John L. Buck, Land Utilization in China, p. 319.

B. 1950-1958

Year	Prices received by farmers (1950 = 100)	Prices paid by farmers (industrial products) (1950 = 100)	Scissors differential (1930-1936 average = 100)
1950	100	100	131.8
1951	119.6	110.3	124.4
1952	121.6	109.7	121.8
1953	133.9	108.2	109.6
1954	138.4	110.3	109.2
1955	137.7	111.9	113.3
1956	141.8	110.8	107.0
1957	148.8	112.1	103.0
1958	152.1	111.4	—

Source: Dwight Perkins, Market Control and Planning in Communist China, p. 234.

Table 8 (continued)

Note: Perkins used official data on prices and the terms of
trade to compile this table. He presents several partial checks
which indicate that the official data are not out of line with independent price observations. The comparison with the 1930s
remains somewhat tenuous, however, and it is possible that
the terms of trade in 1950 were more disadvantageous to the
peasants compared to the 1930-1936 period than the above
index indicates. The steady shift after 1950 in favor of agriculture, however, is not in question.

Table 9

Peasant Labor-Day Inputs in Chinese Agriculture

Year	Average annual labor days (days)	Total annual labor days (billions of days)
1950	119.0	26.489
1951	119.0	26.835
1952	119.0	27.168
1953	119.0	27.537
1954	119.3	28.155
1955	121.0	29.439
1956	149.0	38.084
1957	159.5	41.518
1958	174.6	47.474
1959	189.0	58.420

Source: Peter Schran, The Development of Chinese Agriculture 1950-1959, p. 75.

Note: The sharp increases from the large-scale mobiliza-
tions for rural water conservancy in the winters of 1955-1956
and 1957-1958 are reflected above. The estimates cited for
1959 appear somewhat improbable as demobilization was proceeding throughout the year.

Selected bibliography

Agrarian China: Selected Source Materials from Chinese
   Authors. London, 1939. (Compiled and translated by the
   research staff of the Secretariat, Institute of Pacific
   Relations.)
Bank of China. An Analysis of Shanghai Commodity Prices
   1923-1932. Shanghai, 1933.
Baran, Paul A. The Political Economy of Growth. New
   York, 1962.
Barnett, Robert W. Economic Shanghai: Hostage to Politics
   1937-41. New York, 1941.
Bronfenbrenner, Martin. "The Appeal of Confiscation in Eco-
   nomic Development." The Economics of Underdevelop-
   ment. Ed. A. N. Agarwala and S. P. Singh. New York, 1963.
Buck, John Lossing. Agricultural Survey of Szechuan Prov-
   ince, China. Chungking, 1943.
_____. Chinese Farm Economy. Chicago, 1930.
_____. Land Utilization in China: A study of 16,786 farms
   in 168 localities, and 38,256 farm families in twenty-two
   provinces in China, 1929-1933. 3 vols. Chicago, 1937.
   (Page references in the text are to a reprint [New York,
   1968] of the first edition, vol. 1, published in Nanking,
   1937.)
_____. Some Basic Agricultural Problems of China. New
   York, 1947.
Chang, John. "Industrial Development of China 1912-49."

Journal of Economic History XXVII (March 1967): 56-81.

Chang, Kia-ngau. The Inflationary Spiral: The Experience in China, 1939-1950. New York, 1958.

Chang, Yu-i, ed. Chung-kuo chin-tai nung-yeh shih tzu-liao, ti-san-chi, 1927-1937 [Materials on China's modern agricultural history, Vol. 3, 1927-1937]. Peking, 1957.

Chao, Kang. The Rate and Pattern of Industrial Growth in Communist China. Ann Arbor, 1965.

Chao, Kuo-chun. Agrarian Policy of the Chinese Communist Party 1921-1959. Bombay and New York, 1960.

Chen, Han-seng. Landlord and Peasant in China. New York, 1936.

_____. The Present Agrarian Problem in China. Shanghai, 1933.

Chen, Nai-ruenn. Chinese Economic Statistics: A Handbook for Mainland China. Chicago, 1967.

Chen, P. T. Recent Financial Developments in China. Nanking, 1936.

Chen, Po-ta. A Study of Land Rent in Pre-Liberation China. Peking, 1966.

Cheng, Chu-yuan. Communist China's Economy 1949-1962: Structural Changes and Crisis. South Orange, New Jersey, 1963.

_____. Income and Standard of Living in Mainland China. 2 vols. Hong Kong, 1957.

Cheng, Yu-kwei. Foreign Trade and Industrial Development of China. Washington, D.C., 1956.

China, People's Republic of. Agrarian Reform Law of the People's Republic of China. Peking, 1950. (Promulgated June 30, 1950.)

_____. Ten Great Years. Peking, 1960.

China, Republic of. Ministry of Industries. Bureau of Foreign Trade. China Industrial Handbooks: Chekiang. Shanghai, 1935.

_____. China Industrial Handbooks: Kiangsu. Shanghai, 1933.

_____. Hunan: An Economic Survey. Shanghai, 1936.

China Handbook 1937-45. New York, 1947.

The China Year Book 1934. Shanghai, 1934.

The China Year Book 1935. Shanghai, 1935.

The China Year Book 1936. Shanghai, 1936.

Chou, Shun-hsin. The Chinese Inflation 1937-1949. New York, 1963.

Doi, Akira. "The Present Situation of Agricultural Collectivization in China." Asian Affairs II (March 1957): 47-62.

Donnithorne, Audrey. China's Economic System. London, 1967.

Ecklund, George N. Financing the Chinese Government Budget: Mainland China 1950-1959. Chicago, 1966.

Eckstein, Alexander. The National Income of Communist China. New York, 1961.

Fei, Hsiao-tung. Peasant Life in China: A Field Study of Country Life in the Yangtze Valley. London, 1939.

_____, and Chang, Chih-I. Earthbound China: A Study of Rural Economy in Yunnan. Chicago, 1945.

_____, and Chow, Yung-teh. China's Gentry. Chicago, 1968.

Feuerwerker, Albert. The Chinese Economy, 1912-1949. Michigan Papers in Chinese Studies No. 1. Ann Arbor, 1968.

_____. "Materials for the Study of the Economic History of Modern China." Journal of Economic History XXI (March 1961): 41-60.

Fong, H. D. "Bibliography on the Land Problems of China." Nankai Social and Economic Quarterly III (July 1935): 325-384.

Fukutake, Tadashi. Asian Rural Society: China, India, Japan. Tokyo, 1967.

Gamble, Sidney D. North China Villages: Social, Political and Economic Activities Before 1933. Berkeley, 1963.

_____. Ting Hsien: A North China Rural Community. Stanford, 1968.

Ganguli, B. N. "An Analysis of New China's Agrarian Reform Law." Indian Economic Review I (February 1953): 14-32.

_____. "Reorganization of Chinese Agriculture after Land Reform." Indian Economic Review I (August 1953): 22-44.

Hinton, William. Fanshen: A Documentary of Revolution in a
    Chinese Village. New York, 1966.
Ho, Kan-chih. A History of the Modern Chinese Revolution.
    Peking, 1959.
Ho, Ping-ti. Studies on the Population of China, 1368-1953.
    Cambridge, Mass., 1959.
Hollister, William W. China's Gross National Product and
    Social Accounts, 1950-1957. Glencoe, Ill., 1958.
Hou, Chi-ming. "Economic Dualism: The Case of China, 1840-
    1937." Journal of Economic History XXIII (September
    1963): 277-297.
_____. Foreign Investment and Economic Development in
    China 1840-1937. Cambridge, Mass., 1965.
_____. "Some Reflections on the Economic History of Modern
    China (1840-1949)." Journal of Economic History XXIII
    (December 1963): 595-605.
Hughes, T. J., and Luard, D. E. T. The Economic Development
    of Communist China, 1949-60. London, 1961.
Ishikawa, Shigeru. "Agrarian Reform and its Productivity
    Effect: Implication of the Chinese Pattern." Paper de-
    livered at the International Conference on the Structure
    and Development in Asian Economies. Tokyo, September
    9-14, 1968.
_____. "An Analysis of Economic Growth in China." Asian
    Affairs II (March 1957): 21-46.
_____. Economic Development in Asian Perspective.
    Tokyo, 1967.
_____. National Income and Capital Formation in Mainland
    China: An Examination of Official Statistics. Tokyo, 1965.
_____. "Resource Flow between Agriculture and Industry:
    The Chinese Experience." The Developing Economies V
    (March 1967): 3-49.
Jones, Edwin F. "Comments on Chinese Growth Trends 1952-
    1965." The ASTE Bulletin (Association for the Study of
    Soviet-Type Economies) VII (Winter 1965): 11-14.
_____. "The Emerging Pattern of China's Economic Revolu-

tion." An Economic Profile of Mainland China. Washington, D.C., 1967. (Studies prepared for the Joint Economic
Committee, U.S. Congress.)

_____. "The Role of Developmental Policies and Economic
Organization in Innovation and Growth: Communist China."
An Economic Profile of Mainland China. Washington, D.C.,
1967. (Studies prepared for the Joint Economic Committee, U.S. Congress.)

Kuan, Ta-tung. The Socialist Transformation of Capitalist
Industry and Commerce in China. Peking, 1960.

Larsen, Marion R. "China's Agriculture Under Communism."
An Economic Profile of Mainland China. Washington, D.C.,
1967. (Studies prepared for the Joint Economic Committee, U.S. Congress.)

Lewis, W. Arthur. "Economic Development with Unlimited
Supplies of Labour." The Economics of Underdevelopment.
Ed. A. N. Agarwala and S. P. Singh. New York, 1963.

_____. "Unlimited Labour: Further Notes." The Manchester
School XXVI (January 1958): 1-32.

Li, Choh-ming. Economic Development of Communist China:
An Appraisal of the First Five Years of Industrialization.
Berkeley, 1959.

_____. The Statistical System of Communist China. Berkeley
and Los Angeles, 1962.

Liao, Lu-yen. "The Great Victory in Land Reform During the
Past Three Years." New China's Economic Achievements
1949-52. Comp. China Committee for the Promotion of
International Trade. Peking, 1952.

Lieu, D. K. China's Economic Stabilization and Reconstruction. New Brunswick, New Jersey, 1948.

Liu, Shao-chi. "On the Agrarian Reform Law." The Agrarian
Reform Law of the People's Republic of China. Peking,
1950.

Liu, Ta-chung. China's National Income 1931-36: An Exploratory Study. Washington, D.C., 1946.

_____. "The Tempo of Economic Development of the Chinese

Mainland, 1949-1965." An Economic Profile of Mainland
China. Washington, D.C., 1967. (Studies prepared for the
Joint Economic Committee, U.S. Congress.)
_____, and Kung-chia, Yeh. The Economy of the Chinese
Mainland: National Income and Economic Development
1933-1959. Princeton, 1965.
Mah, Feng-hwa. "The Financing of Public Investment in Com-
munist China." Journal of Asian Studies XXI (November
1961): 38-48.
Minami Manshū Tetsudō Kabushiki Kaisha, Chōsabu [South
Manchurian Railway Company, Research Division].
Hokushi nōson gaikyō chōsa hōkoku: Chang-teh Hsien,
Honan. [Report on the agricultural situation in north
China: Chang-teh Hsien, Honan]. Tokyo, 1940.
Minami Manshū Tetsudō Kabushiki Kaisha, Hokushi Keizai
Chōsajō [South Manchurian Railway Company, North
China Economic Research Institute]. Hokushi nōson
gaikyō chōsa hōkoku. Vol. II: Tai-an Hsien, Shantung.
[Report on the agricultural situation in north China.
Vol. II: Tai-an Hsien, Shantung]. Dairen, 1940.
Miyashita, Tadao. The Currency and Financial System of
Mainland China. Tokyo, 1966.
Myrdal, Jan. Report from a Chinese Village. New York, 1965.
Nankai Institute of Economics, Nankai University. Nankai
Index Numbers, 1934. Tientsin, 1935.
Nurkse, Ragnar. Problems of Capital Formation in Underde-
veloped Countries. New York, 1964.
Ou, Pao-san. "A New Estimate of China's National Income."
Journal of Political Economy LIV (December 1946):
547-54.
_____. Chung-kuo kuo-min so-te i-chiu-san-san nien
[China's National Income, 1933]. 2 vols. Shanghai, 1937.
(Author's name also romanized as "Wu.")
Perkins, Dwight H. Market Control and Planning in Communist
China. Cambridge, Mass., 1966.
Po, Yi-po. "Three Years of Achievements of the People's

Republic of China." New China's Economic Achievements
1949-52. Comp. China Committee for the Promotion of
International Trade. Peking, 1952.

Raup, Philip M. "Land Reform and Agricultural Development."
Agricultural Development and Economic Growth. Ed.
Herman M. Southworth and Bruce F. Johnston, Ithaca, 1967.

Remer, Charles F. Foreign Investments in China. New York, 1933.

Robinson, Claude. Understanding Profits. Princeton, 1961.

Robinson, Joan. An Essay on Marxian Economics. London, 1963.

Schran, Peter. The Development of Chinese Agriculture,
1950-1959. Urbana, Ill., 1969.

Schultz, Theodore. Transforming Traditional Agriculture.
New Haven, 1964.

Schurmann, Franz. Ideology and Organization in Communist
China. Berkeley, 1966.

Silver and Prices in China. Shanghai, 1935. (Report of the
committee established by the Ministry of Industries for
the study of silver values and commodity prices.)

Sun, Kungtu C. The Economic Development of Manchuria in
the First Half of the Twentieth Century. Assisted by
Ralph W. Huenemann. Cambridge, Mass., 1969.

Tang, Anthony M. "Policy and Performance in Agriculture."
Economic Trends in Communist China. Ed. Alexander
Eckstein, Walter Galenson, and Ta-chung Liu. Chicago, 1968.

Tawney, R. H. Land and Labour in China. London, 1932.

Teng, Tse-hui. The Outstanding Success of the Agrarian Reform Movement in China. Peking, 1954.

Thomas, S. B. Recent Political and Economic Developments
in China. New York, 1950.

Walker, Kenneth R. "Collectivisation in Retrospect: The
'Socialist High Tide' of Autumn 1955-Spring 1956." The
China Quarterly, April-June 1966, pp. 1-43.

_____. "Organization for Agricultural Production." Econom-
ic Trends in Communist China. Ed. A. Eckstein, W. Galenson, and T. C. Liu. Chicago, 1968.

_____. Planning in Chinese Agriculture: Socialisation and

the Private Sector 1956-1962. Chicago, 1965.

Warriner, Doreen. Land Reform in Principle and Practice. Oxford, 1969.

Wu, Yuan-li. An Economic Survey of Communist China. New York, 1956.

Yang, C. K. Chinese Communist Society: The Family and the Village. Cambridge, Mass., 1965. (Originally published as two separate works: The Chinese Family in the Communist Revolution and A Chinese Village in Early Communist Transition.)

Yen, Chung-p'ing, ed. Chung-kuo chin-tai ching-chi shih t'ung-chi tzu-liao hsüan-chi [Selected statistical materials on China's modern economic history]. Peking, 1955.

Yin, Helen, and Yin, Yi-chang. Economic Statistics of Mainland China (1949-1957). Cambridge, Mass., 1960.

Young, Arthur N. China's Wartime Finance and Inflation 1937-1945. Cambridge, Mass., 1965.

Young, John. The Research Activities of the South Manchurian Railway Company, 1907-1945: A History and Bibliography. New York, 1966.

Index

About the author

Victor D. Lippit is Assistant Professor of Economics and Chairman of the Asian Studies Program at the University of California, Riverside.

A graduate of Harvard College, Professor Lippit did his graduate work at Yale University, where he received his Ph.D. in 1971. In 1967/68 he was a Research Associate at Hitotsubashi University in Tokyo, and in 1972/73 he was a Postdoctoral Fulbright Reseach Fellow at Tokyo University.

In the summer of 1972 Professor Lippit was a member of the first delegation of American economists to visit China.